Puerto Rico

Berlitz Publishing Company, Inc.

Princeton   Mexico City   Dublin   Eschborn   Singapore

Berlitz Trademark Reg. U.S. Patent Office and other countries
Marca Registrada

Original Text:	revised by Lindsay Bennett; original text by Ken Bernstein and Don Larrimore
Editor:	Christopher Billy
Photography:	Pete Bennett; Kurt Ammann, pages 46, 80-81, 82
Cover Photo:	Pete Bennett
Photo Editor:	Naomi Zinn
Layout:	Media Content Marketing, Inc.
Cartography:	Ortelius Design

Although the publisher tries to insure the accuracy of all the information in this book, changes are inevitable and errors may result. The publisher cannot be responsible for any resulting loss, inconvenience, or injury. If you find an error in this guide, please let the editors know by writing to Berlitz Publishing Company, 400 Alexander Park, Princeton, NJ 08540-6306.

ISBN 2-8315-7225-8
Revised 1999 – First Printing December 1999

Printed in Singapore
019/912 REV

CONTENTS

● A (☛ in the text denotes a highly recommended sight

Puerto Rico

PUERTO RICO AND ITS PEOPLE

Now at the crossroad between Latin America and North America, Puerto Rico was once the eastern gateway to the Spanish New World and one of the most strategically important islands in the world. Lying where the Atlantic meets the Caribbean, Puerto Rico is 1,000 miles (1,600 km) southeast of Miami and 1,600 miles (2,560 km) from New York. It measures 110 miles (176 km) and is 36 miles (58 km) at its widest point from north to south. The easternmost and smallest of the Greater Antilles, Puerto Rico is between the Dominican Republic (to the west) and the Virgin Islands (to the east).

For such a small island, Puerto Rico is blessed with remarkable diversity: beautiful sandy beaches wrap around its coastline; coral reefs sit only a little way offshore. The flat coastal plain proved ideal for development and for agriculture—most of the major towns are within a few kilometers of the sea, as are acres and acres of banana, plantain, and pineapple farms. The interior is marked by higher ground: verdant pastures, stark hills, waterfalls, and an eerily primitive rain forest.

The El Yunque rain forest in the northeast is battered by the passing trade winds and receives over twice as much rain as the western part of the island. This ancient tropical wetland forest has been protected since the 18th century; its many waterfalls and streams nourish the crops on the coastal plains.

Other, dryer forests in the east cover a layer of limestone rock that over the millennia has eroded to produce remarkable cave systems and distinctive "waves" of small hills. Desert or dry forests extend inland from the coastal fringes of the south, where rainfall is sparse, and mangroves surround the salt flats at the mouths of rivers and inlets, providing protective habitats

for thousands of seabirds and marine creatures. Several national and state parks (*bosques nacionales* and *estatales*) are devoted to protecting the island's diverse natural environments.

Such a wealth of natural features is rare in the Caribbean islands, but this abundance was of little consequence when Columbus first set eyes on Puerto Rico in 1493. Under orders from the Spanish crown to search for gold and other treasures to add to the royal coffers, Columbus claimed the island for Spain but then left toward South America. The Indians he discovered living here, the Taínos, were more aware of the bounty that nature had bestowed on them—they lived quiet, organized lives, growing crops and fishing.

Puerto Rico's police force is well-outfitted to weave through the city crowds.

The same trade winds that brought Columbus to the Indies cool the island air and push the clouds about in an unending spectacle. Temperatures vary only slightly year-round, with the monthly averages ranging from 75° to 81°F (22°–26°C). Except for a dry season in the spring, rain showers occur frequently, but they're usually short and sweet. The only blot on the horizon is the occasional hurricane—the Taínos feared this untamable spirit, which seemed to come from nowhere; today's forecasting methods enable residents, and visitors, to better prepare for these huge storms.

The Spanish conquistadors put the Taínos to work on plantations. Many died of disease and the harsh conditions; African slaves were eventually imported to take their place. Puerto Rico was not as profitable as other Caribbean islands in terms of agricultural output, but it became an important staging post for ships traveling between the gold mines of South America and Madrid; it was also named the Roman Catholic Church's see, or seat of power, in the New World. These responsibilities allowed Puerto Rico to live up to its name—"rich port." With time it became a prize sought after by many European crowns, and by pirate forces.

Every major city in the New World had a military garrison, but when the Spanish decided to fortify the capital of

The city walls around Old San Juan once kept its citizens alive—and now does the same for their compelling history.

Puerto Rico, San Juan, they created a masterpiece. The earliest fortress, La Fortaleza, was joined by mighty El Morro, built to guard the entrance to the port. Fort San Cristóbal was built to defend the landward approaches. These were then connected by a 40-ft (12-m) high wall that entirely circled the city. Although parts of the southern and eastern sections of the wall were demolished early in the 19th century to allow the city to expand, Old San Juan and its fortifications have been miraculously well-preserved.

The Spanish ruled Puerto Rico for 300 years, creating a little slice of Spain in the Caribbean—you'll see touches of Madrid or Seville in the style of the older houses. In 1898, however, the Spanish went to war with the United States over neighboring Cuba. They suffered an embarrassing defeat, and in the negotiations that followed, Puerto Rico (along with the Philippines) became a territory of the US. Today Puerto Rico is a Commonwealth (*Estado Libre Asociado* in Spanish) of the United States. Most of today's population seem to be content with the arrangement, as the 1951 Constitution allows a great deal of self-government, and the island is certainly not a clone of its benevolent big brother.

Puerto Rican society today is a fascinating mix of Amerindian, European, African, and American ideas and influences. Although many tourists are drawn by the old—the historical forts, streets, and buildings preserved for posterity—their visits bring them into contact with a living society that is vital, energetic, and evolving. Whatever their genetic heritage, Puerto Ricans consider Spanish to be their mother tongue (though you may also hear a good deal of "Spanglish," the result of migrations to the United States and back again).

Puerto Ricans have a palpable zest for life. They are a social people—chatting from open windows, on street corners, and across lines of moving traffic. Conversation is always loud and animated—be it a political debate or a discussion about a latest boyfriend.

Although deeply religious, Puertorriqueños have a love of earthly pleasures. Music is ever-present, the air filled with salsas and merengues coming from apartment windows, shopfronts, and passing cars. The beat of African drums accompanying Spanish guitars is infectious, and it won't be long before your toes start tapping and your body starts swaying.

The older generation, perhaps thinking wistfully about days gone by, watches the young as they have fun. The men enjoy watching the young ladies pass, and the

There's always time for a quick game and a long chat in Puerto Rico's town squares.

ladies coo over every new addition to the family. Everyone visits Grandma after church on Sundays.

The Spanish ritual of taking an evening stroll is alive and well in Puerto Rico: the *paseo* takes place around the plazas of towns and along the grassy approach leading to El Morro. The latest generation has transformed this tradition into cruising by car, repeating a circuit around Old San Juan or along Ashford Avenue in Condado, to show off their prized automobiles. The young city-dwellers, with a penchant for designer clothes and being "in vogue," are beginning to break some of the traditional ways. Surrounded by McDonald's and cable TV since birth, they are able to embrace almost anything American and make it their own. The traditional chaperone has lost her job as young people court in the modern American way. Many young Puertorriqueños leave in search of new pastures, to explore the world of opportunity that the mainland US has to offer. The country dwellers are also on the move, leaving the land and searching for opportunities in the ever-growing cities. The *jíbaro,* or country farmer, with his straw hat and machete—long a symbol of the "salt-of-the-earth" Puerto Rican—is disappearing fast, and there are worries about how this will effect the future.

On the other hand, the *West Side Story* generation has now reached retirement age, and many older Puerto Ricans who have lived for decades in New York and other cities in the States are now returning to their homeland. They play domi-

noes in the village squares, smiling about the irony that this simple rhythm of passing the days was part of the reason they left all those years ago. Life comes full circle, and these individuals, who have had the chance to experience so much more, now revel in their island's heritage and traditional lifestyle in a way that will keep Puerto Rico fresh and vibrant well into the future.

Cobblestone streets and quiet corners foster the romance of Puerto Rico.

A BRIEF HISTORY

The First Puerto Ricans

The island's earliest known inhabitants, Indians now called Arcaícos ("the ancients"), were primitive fishermen. More than 2,000 years ago they were conquered by another tribe called the Igneri who had mastered farming and pottery-making. The final stage of Indian advancement began while Europe was in the Middle Ages: the Taíno Indians, a peaceful people native to Venezuela, traveled up through the chain of the Lesser Antilles and settled the island they called Borinquén. They lived in thatched houses, hunted and farmed, and worked ceramics and textiles with great skill. Several of their ceremonial "ball courts," which were used for certain social

The recently-unearthed "ball courts" at Tibes Indian Ceremonial Park are an important vestige of the Taíno.

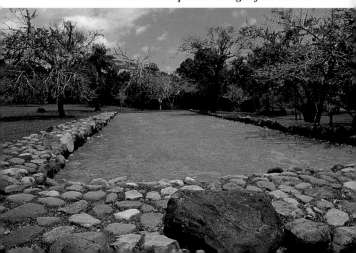

or religious gatherings, have been discovered throughout Puerto Rico. The Taínos feared an evil spirit, Juracán, who was responsible for violent storms and gave his name to the tropical hurricanes of the West Indies. They also feared an earthly evil: the Carib Indians, who periodically raided their land for loot and captives. The Taínos' fears were well founded. The word "cannibal" derives from Carib, a reminder of the way these marauders disposed of some prisoners.

The Arrival of the Europeans

On 19 November 1493, Columbus was lucky enough to be met by the kindly Taínos (in fact, the name Taíno meant "friend" and was used by the Indians to enable the Europeans to distinguish between them and the not-so-friendly Caribs). The Taínos were the ones who introduced the Spanish to tobacco, corn on the cob, and that archetypal Caribbean mode of relaxation, the hammock.

Columbus christened the island San Juan Bautista (honoring St. John the Baptist). It was the first colonist, Juan Ponce de León, who, admiring a bay on the north coast, declared it Puerto Rico ("rich port"). Sixteenth-century mapmakers back in Spain mistakenly confused the names, so that in the end the port became San Juan and the whole island was called a "rich port"; once on the maps, the names stuck.

A less innocent error was an American attempt to erase four centuries of Spanish history. After the conquest of 1898 the first US military governor ordered that the name be spelled Porto Rico. This semi-Italian corruption didn't last long. Today some nationalists still yearn for good old Borinquén, a name you'll see on many restaurants and bars.

Ponce de León had received permission to found a Spanish colony on the island in 1508. For reasons of security, he settled a few miles inland from what is now San Juan. The site was swampy and mosquito-ridden, and, after a number of outbreaks of disease, his fellow colonists abandoned him and moved to the future capital city. They immediately began work on the formidable fortifications for which the city is still famous. Ponce de León also suffered another setback. He became involved in a power struggle with Columbus's son, Diego, who through his father's will had claims on the island. The small colony could not cope with the egos of two such powerful men. The Spanish crown solved the tense standoff by entrusting Ponce de León with another voyage of exploration. His search resulted in the discovery of Florida.

Ponce de León, first colonist on what is now Puerto Rico, is honored in Plaza San José.

While on a second expedition to colonize Florida, in 1521, Ponce de León was critically wounded during an attack by Indians; the explorer hoped to return Puerto Rico but lost his fight for life on the way back, in Havana, Cuba.

Ponce de León's successors imagined that the island was one big gold mine and set the Indians to work mining and panning. They were wrong, however: the gold soon ran out. The Spaniards then looked to agriculture to turn a profit and began growing sugar cane, which had been introduced to the

Caribbean on Columbus's second journey. As the number of Taíno and Carib laborers declined, due to disease and suicide, plantation owners eventually began importing slaves from West Africa.

Puerto Rico quickly developed into a major port and trading post—it was one of the last major ports Spanish galleons stopped in before sailing back to the motherland. San Juan also became the center for the Catholic Church's evangelization of the New World; numerous churches, convents, and monasteries were established throughout the island to aid in this effort.

A Beleaguered Island

To the pirates and privateers who sailed the Caribbean in the early 16th century, the fortress of El Morro at San Juan represented the might, and the wealth, of the Spanish Crown. Lured by the promise of treasure galleons and stores of ammunition, some pirates worked independently; others, however, were employed by the various European crowns, particularly the British, to help carry on their power struggles in the colonial world. Puerto Rico suffered from constant attacks. The most poignant, though not typical, case involved raids against the coastal hamlet of San Germán. Two French pirate ships first ravaged the village in 1528. It happened again in 1538 and three times in the following five years. After every attack the settlers put out the fires, buried the dead, and rebuilt San Germán. In 1554, after the sixth sacking, the settlers decided to move inland to the town's present hilltop location. With remarkable persistence the pirates climbed all the way, twice, just to pillage San Germán.

More ominous than the French were the forces of Sir Francis Drake. The great British navigator and adventurer operated in the Caribbean for years before he turned his attention to Puerto Rico. In 1595 Drake learned that a 2-million-peso

Sixteenth-century El Morro simultaneously advertised Spanish wealth and held off the pirates who wished to obtain it.

gold shipment had just arrived in San Juan aboard a Spanish galleon. This kind of booty was worth a battle, even though Drake knew the city was well protected by a set of forts. The British fleet dueled with the guns of El Morro fort and the defending warships in a long, costly battle. Then, under cover of darkness, Drake sent out attack boats to destroy the Spanish frigates. But light from the burning ships gave El Morro's shore batteries a fine view of their target. The English slunk away without the loot. It was the only defeat of Drake's career; within months he was dead.

El Morro was not, however, invulnerable. A few years later, a British fleet commanded by George Clifford, the Earl of Cum-

Columbus's first landing on the island is grandly memorialized in the town of Aguada.

berland, shrewdly outflanked the fortress. Far outnumbered by the 1,700-man invasion force, the defenders of El Morro surrendered after a two-week siege. But the English flag did not fly over San Juan for long. Four hundred of Cumberland's troops died in an epidemic of yellow fever and dysentery, and the British had to withdraw less than three months after their victory. The Dutch were the next to try: in 1625, they succeeded in pinning the Spanish into the confines of El Morro; but after looting everything of value, they set fire to San Juan and departed. Because surrender was never considered, the Spanish—and today's Puerto Ricans—regard this episode as a victory.

Soon after this, the Spanish began building a thick defensive wall all around San Juan. With an average height of 40 feet (12 m), it was a formidable site, and is still one of the most impressive parts of the old city. It seems to have impressed generations of marauders; once it was complete, they stayed away for more than 150 years.

A final British rally against Puerto Rico came in 1797. Seven thousand troops under Sir Ralph Abercromby landed east of San Juan and blockaded the city. For two weeks the battle see-sawed. Finally, as suddenly and unexpectedly as they had arrived, the British retired. According to one version, it was all because of St. Ursula and the 11,000 Virgins. On the last night of the siege, devout local women, led by their bishop, marched through the streets of old San Juan in a torchlight parade praying for deliverance. The legend says General Abercromby heard the church bells tolling, saw the lights, mistakenly deduced that Spanish reinforcements had arrived, and fled.

The End of Spanish Rule

For Spain the 19th century was a bitter slide from imperial might to the status of a has-been. By the early 1800s independence movements had overthrown Spanish rule in most of the Western Hemisphere. Madrid's most important remaining possessions were the island colonies of Cuba and Puerto Rico, both of which were chafing under the yoke of colonial rule and the bitter system of slavery. To squash subversive ideas about independence in Puerto Rico, Madrid imposed ruthless military control. The most memorable incident occurred in 1868 in the mountain town of Lares, when government forces crushed an uprising of secessionists, killing or jailing the insurgents, and many innocent victims. The event is remembered as *El Grito de Lares* (the cry of Lares).

The colonial government could not, however, hold back the tide of change sweeping the Caribbean. In 1872, one momentous decree abolished the 350-year-old institution of slavery in Puerto Rico, and in 1897 Spain cut the colonial ties and finally granted the island autonomy. The long dream of independence seemed to have come true. But eight months after Madrid had authorized home rule for Puerto Rico, American troops arrived to take it away.

The Spanish-American War was no great challenge for the US force that landed at Guánica, on Puerto Rico's calm south coast, rather than at fortified San Juan. Military resistance was spotty at best. By starting at the soft underbelly, the 16,000 troops of General Nelson A. Miles gained control of the island in less than three weeks. The central issue that had drawn Spain and the United States into war—Cuba's struggle for independence—was resolved in that island's favor: Cuba's freedom was guaranteed by the Paris Treaty of 1898. But Spain's two other major colonies, the Philippines and Puerto Rico, simply changed hands, becoming colonies of the United States.

Puerto Rico and the United States

The population was initially little better off under its new landlord. Most Puerto Ricans were tied to the large agricultural companies—they lived in company houses and were paid in tokens that could only be spent at company stores. They didn't starve, but they didn't thrive, either. A few strong voices were eventually raised: some proposed radical action while others advocated working within the system for a more democratic society. One especially prominent activist was Muñoz Marín Rivera, who is credited with helping to move Puerto Rico toward the 20th century.

Washington gradually began to grant Puerto Ricans a greater degree of self-government and representation. In 1900 the first civil governor was appointed (all the appointed governors were Americans until 1946). In 1917 Puerto Ricans won a mixed bag of benefits: they were given more say in their internal affairs, made citizens of the United States—and declared eligible for conscription in World War I. In the years between the World Wars there were continued efforts to change the island's status and improve its quality of life. Some, such as those who followed radical Pedro Albizu Cam-

Historical Landmarks

1,000 B.C.	Igneri Indians conquer the Arcaícos (the "ancients") and begin farming.
c 700 A.D.	Taíno Indians settle the island; they call it Borinquén.
1493	Columbus claims the island for Spain, naming it San Juan Bautista.
1508	Juan Ponce de León given royal assent to establish a colony on the island.
1521	The city of San Juan is founded.
1500s & 1600s	San Juan suffers from raids by pirates and colonial powers, but is retained by the Spanish.
1868	Secessionist uprising at Lares.
1872	Slavery is abolished by the Spanish.
1897	Spain declares its intention to grant independence.
1898	American troops invade Puerto Rico during the Spanish American War.
1899	The territory is given to the United States at the end of the war.
1900	First US Governor of Puerto Rico appointed.
1917	Puerto Ricans become US citizens.
1940s	"Operation Bootstrap" expands Puerto Rican industry, education, and health and welfare benefits.
1951	Voters approve a new constitution that grants Puerto Rico the status of semi-autonomous commonwealth of the US.
1960s	Tourism expands greatly after the Cuban blockade is imposed.
1996	Tax incentives introduced under Operation Bootstrap are canceled by the Clinton administration.
1998	Referendum for US statehood is defeated.

A skyline view of Old San Juan's carefully preserved historic homes and public buildings.

pos, took to violence, which resulted in several assassinations, though many more insurgents worked within the system.

More Puerto Rican draftees went to war in 1941. Even while poverty lingered from the Great Depression, World War II caused continued hardship on the island because of its isolation in a dangerous sea. But the 1940s saw the emergence of two great political figures: Luis Muñoz Marín, son of Muñoz Marín Rivera and founder of the new Popular Democratic Party, and Rexford Guy Tugwell, Governor of Puerto Rico from 1941 to 1946. These two men were instrumental in orchestrating an amazing economic expansion that almost single-handedly converted the island from an underdeveloped backwater into a pace-setting industrial society. Under "Operation Bootstrap," which attracted hundreds of new factories to Puerto Rico through tax and other incentives, the per-capita income soared to the highest in Latin America. Life expectancy rose from about 45 years in 1940 to an enviable 71 years today. Pouring one-third of its entire budget into education, Puerto Rico cut illiteracy to about 10 percent.

The Commonwealth of Puerto Rico

Politically, recent history is less conclusive. In 1951 the island's voters approved a new constitution (still in effect) forming a commonwealth between the United States and the "free associated state" of Puerto Rico (though even the commencement ceremony was marred by violent demonstrations by radicals). As a result Puerto Ricans now elect their own governor, legislature, and local officials, and send a non-voting representative to the US Congress. In turn, Washington runs the postal, customs, and immigration services, handles defense and foreign relations, and sends dollars—particularly useful in times of crisis, such as after hurricanes.

In recent elections, power has alternated between parties backing the status-quo and those preferring even closer ties with the United States, though a referendum in 1998 defeated a move towards statehood. A third force is often in the news, but the parties pushing for independence—establishing Puerto Rico as a separate nation—have thus far gained only minority support at the polls. The withdrawal of tax incentives for US companies operating in Puerto Rico by the Clinton administration in 1996, which has caused job losses and economic hardship, is another thorn in the side of those who hope for a stronger and more self-sufficient society. On the other hand, tourism, which began in earnest in the 1960s, brings increasing numbers of visitors—and amounts of money—to the island's economy.

WHERE TO GO

Puerto Rico is an island of contrasts, perhaps the only destination in the Caribbean where the city streets hold as much allure as the beaches. One third of the island's population of just over three million live in San Juan, which is undoubtedly the draw for many. One of the leading commercial and industrial centers of the Caribbean, it is characterized by high-rise office blocks and sprawling suburbs. It's the delights and historical treasures of the old town, however, that capture the eyes and imaginations of most visitors. And beyond the limits of the capital are mountains, rivers and lakes, forests, and plantations waiting to be explored.

OLD SAN JUAN

Old San Juan is without doubt one of the most spectacular sights of the Caribbean. Founded in 1521, it is partially sur-

rounded by walls and fortifications that have protected it from modernization and indiscriminate development. The carefully preserved historic houses and public buildings retain many of the most charming features of the original Spanish colonial architecture. Cobblestone streets (the stones were brought as ballast on the Spanish ships,

Plaza de Colón, named after the man who discovered the island 500 years ago.

which went home filled with treasure and gold), tiny squares, and grand plazas surprise visitors at every turn as they wander the neat grid of streets planned four centuries ago.

Only eight blocks wide, San Juan can easily be covered on foot, though there are some steep ascents that may be challenging in the Caribbean heat. Even if you only have one day, you'll be able to enjoy its delights. If possible, however, take at least a couple of days. Enjoying a rest in a shady plaza or taking a long lunch at an outdoor café are just as much a part of your trip as a tour around the museums. San Juan

> **Don't expect the sidewalks to be for people on the move. They are a place for city-dwellers to meet friends, stand to chat, and eat lunch.**

is a living city, and it's especially bustling after dark, when crowds throng to the bars and restaurants or simply stroll the narrow streets and airy plazas.

Begin your exploration at **Plaza de Colón** (Columbus Square). If you take a taxi from the outlying resort areas, this is a good place to alight—before traffic in the narrow streets forces your vehicle to a halt. The square was named after Columbus on the 400th anniversary of Puerto Rico's discovery, in 1893. After admiring the unusually tall statue of the discoverer, leave the square from the northeastern corner and walk along Boulevard del Valle; this is a pretty street with a series of brightly painted buildings, but the traffic can be busy.

At the top of the hill, on the right, you'll find the towering walls of **Fuerte San Cristóbal**, the largest fort in Puerto Rico. It's also the youngest fort on the island, built in the 18th century to plug a hole in the easterly defenses of the city. From atop the brick walls, which withstood fierce attacks by cannonballs and other projectiles, you can enjoy panoramic views out to the east and over San Juan Bay to the modern city. The fort's vast interior courtyard now echoes with the sound of running children rather the marching of soldier's boots, but one dormitory of the old barracks has been re-created, with bunks lining the walls and uniforms hung neatly on pegs. Take the long dark walk to the dungeons to find a faded drawing of a Spanish galleon sketched on the wall by a captain accused of treason.

After visiting the fort continue west along Boulevard del Valle, which becomes Calle Norzagaray. Here you'll be tempted by fine views of the sea; you may even catch sight of a cruise ship sailing gracefully into port. This route sits against the **old city walls**, which were completed in 1785, and from here it is easy to see why the city was thought to be impregnable. Thanks to the high, thick walls and the watchtowers with their distinctive rounded roofs, the residents could be sure that no one would approach unseen.

After a walk of about half a mile you'll find the plain façade of the **Museo de Arte e Historia** (San Juan Museum of Art and History) on your left. Once a major market place for the city, built in 1855, the building now houses a major collection of Puerto Rican art.

Just past the museum, a large, open grassy area comes into view. If you happen to be here on a weekend you'll find thousands of Puerto Rican families out flying kites. This area is the best place to take advantage of the sea breezes, and many kites soar hundreds of feet up in the air. When collisions occur or lines get crossed, jovial banter breaks out between the parties—it's a very social activity. The grassy area, cut by one gravel path, leads to the end of the promontory—and the mighty **Fuerte San Felipe del Morro**, usually simply referred to as "El Morro" (meaning "the headland"). On your right as you walk toward the entrance you'll pass the old city cemetery resting between the walls and the sea. The ornate tombs are still carefully attended and hold the remains of some of Puerto Rico's most illustrious

*The Museum of the Americas preserves all types of Amer-
indian art, such as these elaborate costumes and masks.*

families. The entrance to El Morro is reached across a wide
dry moat, a last defense against attack. Walk through the
huge curved doorway to the heart of the fort.

El Morro was one of the most formidable citadels in the
world. During the 16th and 17th centuries it was one of a ring
of forts that held the key to Spanish power in the Caribbean.
The watchtowers of El Morro look out to sea and inland across
San Juan Bay to the coastal plains beyond. The multilevel defenses made it possible to fire weapons from sea level up to
hundreds of feet above ground. Despite some serious attempts
by English and Dutch forces, the fort was never forcibly taken.

Since 1845 the lighthouse here has provided protection for
ships off the coast; the present light dates from 1908. The old
barracks and ammunition arsenal now house a museum, which
offers an audio-visual presentation about the history of the fort

The Institute of Puerto Rican Culture will soon host a new museum in this lovely space.

(in English and Spanish on alternate half hours).

After exploring the fort, walk back across the grassy lawns. (At the small traffic circle at the end of the driveway you'll find refreshment stalls where you can get a cool drink or snack before moving on.) Young Puertorriqueños have taken to skateboarding and rollerblading on nearby **Plaza del Quartel Ballajá**. They gather every day at this square to compete with their peers and show off their skills to passersby.

To the left is **Cuartel de Ballajá** (Ballajá Barracks), once the major army barracks under Spanish rule and now a significant cultural attraction. The second floor of the building houses the **Museum of the Americas**. The museum's mission is to gather collections of artifacts of Amerindian culture, including folk art, basket-ware from Colombia, and ceremonial masks and costumes from around Central America.

The barracks themselves are also interesting—large open rooms that used to house soldiers and their families face in toward a large court, where drills were carried out. The square now remains eerily quiet (unless a school group is touring the museum).

Opposite the entrance to the Barracks is the long white building that houses the **Institute of Puerto Rican Culture**.

A new museum is planned for this space, but in the meantime temporary art exhibitions display the best of Puerto Rican painting and sculpture.

Follow Calle Beneficencia, the street leading off the right side of the barracks, back towards town. You'll soon come to a small square on your left with a huge totemic sculpture. This is **Plaza del Quinto Centenario** (Quincentenary Square). The sculpture symbolizes the 500 years of Puerto Rico's existence. On close inspection, Amerindian and Spanish themes can be seen, but some elements are a little obscure.

Walk on to reach another small square, **Plaza San José** (San José Square), one of the gems of the city. Situated close to El Morro, it was once one of the most important squares in San Juan. In the center is a statue of Juan Ponce de León in full regalia that was cast in 1797 from the iron of a British cannon, confiscated after their unsuccessful attack on the city. Edged by historic buildings, the square has changed little since the 17th century, except that many of the houses have been converted to restaurants and bars. This is a good place to come after dark and watch the world go by.

> Learn, or re-learn, how to fly a kite. The open grassland in front of El Morro is the place to pick up tips and try your hand.

On the north flank of the square is the Spanish Gothic **Iglesia San José** (San José Church), the second-oldest church in the New World. The plain white façade reflects the sunlight, helping cool the interior. The body of Ponce de León was interred here for over 300 years before being moved to the San Juan Cathedral in 1908. Attached to the church is a large building that was originally a **Dominican Convent**. It was an army barracks until 1966, when it was taken under the auspices of the Institute of Puerto Rican Culture. You can enter the main square and see the three cloistered floors that flank it. Art exhibitions are held here regularly.

On the east side of Plaza San José are two important buildings. In the corner is the **Pablo Casals Museum**, dedicated to the life of the cello virtuoso and composer, who lived the last years of his life in Puerto Rico. Casals was responsible for injecting life back into the classical genre here; he sponsored a classical music festival which still takes place every June. Next to the Casals Museum is the **Casa de los Contrafuertes** (House of the Buttresses), named after the sturdy stone supports that reach out at angles from the walls. It is thought to be the oldest privately owned residence in Old San Juan, dating from the early 18th century. There are two museums on the upper floors: the **Pharmacy Museum**—a complete apothecary's shop with bottles and scales—and above it, the **Museum of Latin American Print**.

Leave Plaza San José via Calle Cristo. Halfway down this street on your left you'll find the **Catedral de San Juan** (San Juan Cathedral). The church dates from 1540, though a comprehensive restoration was carried out in the early 19th century. The interior features pretty *trompe l'oeil* details that add depth to the plain columns and domes. On the northern wall is the tomb of Ponce de León; he shares this place of honor with San Pío, a Catholic martyr whose remains were brought from Rome in 1862.

Pablo Casals, champion of classical music, is memorialized in this museum.

Facing the cathedral is **Plazuela de las Monjas**, a tiny square filled with trees, where courting couples and old folks take advantage of the shade. You may also catch the sound of jingling bells signaling that the local ice-cream seller is around. On the north side of the square is the **El Convento Hotel**, a great place to take a break. The hotel has an interesting history because, as the name suggests, it started life as a convent, in 1651. Unfortunately, as the number of nuns declined, the convent was forced to close, and the building, decaying year by year, played host to the best and busiest brothel in the

The bright altar at Catedral de San Juan, where Ponce de León is entombed.

city. It was also one of the cheapest hotels in town before being rescued and transformed in the early 1990s.

On the western flank of the square you'll find the **Museo del Niño** (Children's Museum). No sterile display cases full of artifacts here! This is an entertaining, hands-on activity center where kids can be kids and yet still have a learning experience. There are four floors of interactive exhibits, including a real dentist's chair where mom or dad can be examined by their offspring, and a giant bubble machine on the upper floor.

Behind the museum are a number of other important attractions. Take Calle las Monjas toward San Juan Bay. After a short distance you'll arrive at the western wall and a small square, **Plazuela de la Rogativa**, with a bronze statue commemorating the torchlight religious procession, or *rogativa,* that saved the city in 1797. It's believed that the lights held by the bishop and the women of the city fooled the British forces in the bay into assuming that Spanish reinforcements had arrived. The British fled empty-handed.

Just a short walk north of the square is the **Casa Blanca** (White House), which for 250 years was the home of the descendants of Ponce de León. Something of a mini-fortress, safe behind its own high wall, the house itself is fascinating—the interior is a museum to life in 16th- and 17th-century San Juan, with many rooms full of period furniture.

Walk back toward the Plazuela de la Rogativa and peer over the city wall, which rises over 100 ft (30½ m) at this

Statue commemorating St. Ursula and the 11,000 virgins, who, by praying for deliverance, scared the British away.

point. The plain façade is broken by the **San Juan Gate**, which was once the only entrance to the city from the old port. The gate was constructed in 1639, and the walls were completed in 1641. Every person who traveled across the Atlantic from Spain would enter through this narrow passage—many would make their way directly to the Cathedral to give thanks for a safe arrival—and all goods were transported through here. The thick wooden doors are an impressive sight; they were locked and guarded each night but now remain open to allow people to stroll along the seafront.

Make your way back to the cathedral along Calle San Juan and turn right once again at Calle Cristo. You'll pass some interesting shops that might tempt you to browse for a while (the designer outlet stores are particularly popular). Turn right at Calle Fortaleza to reach one of the jewels of San Juan: **La Fortaleza**. Now the home of the Governor of Puerto Rico, this fort is in fact a historic monument dating back to 1533. It was the first fortification built by the founders of San Juan and has been in constant use since that time. Of course it has grown over the centuries—you'll find extensions and renovations in the Baroque, Gothic, and Neo-Classic styles. Now a National Historic Site, this fascinating home is full of period furniture. You can tour the house and its extensive gardens, but you must book in advance.

At the southern end of Calle Cristo, at the edge of the city wall, is tiny **Capilla del Cristo**. This chapel was said to have been built in the memory of a young man who, in 1753, raced his horse down Calle Cristo, was unable to stop the animal in time, and fell over the wall to his death. Others say that, in fact, the chapel was built to commemorate the fact that the boy was saved by divine intervention at this very spot. Whichever is true, the chapel now stands as a barrier to any other such mishap.

Parque de las Palomas is aptly named: on any given day, there are crowds of pigeons looking for a friend.

To the left of the chapel is 18th-century **Casa del Libro** (House of Books), a small museum devoted to rare books and the printing and binding arts. Next door is the **Centro Nacional de Artes y Artesanías** (Popular Arts and Crafts Center), a showcase of modern art and crafts managed by the Institute of Puerto Rican Culture. Temporary exhibitions are mounted here, and some items are occasionally made available for purchase.

To the right of the chapel is the entrance to **Parque de las Palomas** (Pigeon Park), clinging to the side of the city wall and a favorite with children. The park can be a little oppressive—it's always a flurry of people and pigeons—but at least pause long enough to admire the panoramic views across San Juan harbor.

Back at Calle Fortaleza, take a right and continue to the intersection of Calle San José. Here you'll pass fascinating small shops selling art and crafts from around the world. Wooden carvings from Asia sit side by side with Haitian native paintings.

Take a left and a block farther down you'll enter **Plaza de Armas**. This was the first central square of Old San Juan, and the City Hall, or **Alcaldía**, still sits on its northern side. The army used to drill here, hence the name (*armas* means weapons, or arms), but today it is simply a place for people to meet and have a coffee, or sit and chat. Workers enjoy picnic lunches here at midday; old people while away the afternoon. The Alcaldía has an interesting interior, with checkerboard marble floors and magnificent chandeliers. It's usually open on weekdays; you can check with the tourist information office on the ground floor as to whether it's OK to wander around.

The Piña Colada

In 1954, barman Ramon Marrero spent over three months perfecting a new cocktail that he hoped would best represent the island of Puerto Rico. After many thousands of attempts, he was satisfied, and the piña colada was born. Since then, millions of these frothy blends have been sipped poolside around the world.

Here is the recipe: try it on the road or back at home:

> 2oz Puerto Rican light rum
> 1oz coconut cream
> 1oz dairy cream
> 6oz pineapple juice
> Half a cup of crushed ice

Blend all ingredients well, pour into an iced glass, and garnish with pineapple and maraschino cherry.

Back on Calle Fortaleza, walk east until you reach the **Casa de Callejón** (House of the Alley) on the corner of Callejón de Capilla. A fine example of an 18th-century house, it is now the **Museum of the Puerto Rican Family**, full of the furniture, toys, and other daily artifacts of a well-to-do San Juan family.

Taking a left out of the museum brings you back to Plaza Colón, from where you can make your way south toward San Juan harbor. Along the way you'll pass **Teatro Tapia** (Tapia Theater) named after Puerto Rican playwright Alejandro Tapia y Rivera. The splendid façade was restored in 1976, the interior remodeled in 1987. The theater hosts regular performances of ballet, dance, and drama, often showcasing works by modern Puerto Rican writers and choreographers.

You can't miss the harbor. Just look for the huge cruise ships, which dwarf the surrounding buildings. The **cruise port** comprises several large jetties, from whence hundreds of passengers disembark on a regular basis. Walk west along the seafront in the direction of the town. Next to the ultramodern cruise-ship wharfs you'll will find the rather down-at-the-heel **commercial ferry jetty**, which caters to the small boats that ply across the harbor to the modern city. Taking one of these little boats is one of the best ways to take in the size of the harbor and the old town. You'll also get to see Puerto Ricans at work, and and play—snacking on *empanadillas* (pastry turnovers filled with meat or cheese) and enjoying salsa music.

Near the ferry dock, across Calle Marina, you'll see the rising edifice of the San Juan Post Office, a magnificent building with Art-Deco features. In front of the post office is a tiny tourist information office, **La Casita**, where you can pick up maps and information.

Continue past the Post Office and the adjoining Plaza de Hostos, which is full of souvenir stalls (and faux designer

The harbor is the place to catch a small boat to modern San Juan (or one of the big ones to destinations worldwide).

watches galore). To the left is the **Arsenal de la Marina**, a fine building with strange Moorish details. Built in 1800, it houses the Fine Arts and Folk Arts departments of the Institute of Puerto Rican Culture. In front of you is the **Paseo de la Princessa**, a smart promenade that has emerged from years of neglect to become *the* place in town to stroll in the evening, or to sit and watch the world go by. A number of new statues and fountains now grace the Paseo. One, named *Raices* (Roots), depicts members of each of the races that have contributed to the modern Puerto Rican mix, surrounded by playful dolphins. **La Princessa**, home of the offices of the Puerto Rico Tourist Company, sits along the Paseo. Originally a prison—this is why it is outside the city walls—it is now a showcase of modern Puerto Rican art.

METROPOLITAN SAN JUAN

Toward the end of the 18th century, the city fathers realized that San Juan was becoming overcrowded, so they decided to break through a section of the vast wall and expand the city's borders. Gangs of laborers were hired to carry out the job (you can see photographs of them in Fuerte San Cristóbal). This action altered the perception that San Juan was a citadel city—already an anachronism at the time— and plans were drawn up to develop the area immediately east of the city, an area that became known as Puerta de Tierra or "gateway to the land." Today, San Juan stretches all the way around the bay. A number of the modern suburbs, though primarily residential, have some interesting attractions for visitors.

Just outside the old town, facing out toward the sea, is the impressive **El Capitolio**, home of the Puerto Rico Legislature. Constructed in 1925, it has already been recognized as a historic monument. Continuing beyond this sight, you'll pass some rather careworn buildings before reaching **Parque Muñoz Rivera,** one of the places where local families like to relax on the weekends. There are areas of formal gardens, a small fort, and children's play area. A seafront promenade to the north sees hundreds of families strolling on warm weekend evenings; the beach, though very narrow, is the nearest one to the old city, and it's always crowded in the afternoon and on weekends.

A series of bridges lead across a small strait to modern San Juan, or to the right to Condado and the resort area.

Miramar, a pleasant residential quarter with fine fami-

El Capitolio (1925), despite its comparative youth, is a historic monument.

ly homes, benefits from its position alongside the Isla Grande commuter airport. **Santurce**, a business and residential area, has few attractions except for a concentration of movie palaces and the **Centro de Bellas Artes**, the largest performing arts center in the Caribbean. Housing three theaters and five rehearsal halls, this complex has spearheaded a resurgence in the popularity of traditional Puerto Rican music and dance. It also has a regular program of performers from around the world.

Hato Rey's unexpected, futuristic skyline marks it as the financial center of the Caribbean. Those skyscrapers are banks, and the street on which they stand has been nicknamed the **Milla de Oro**, or Golden Mile. **Río Piedras** is the home of the University of Puerto Rico. Its considerable campus serves 42,000 students, and the

> **Puerto Rican drivers communicate through a series of imperceptible signs and subtle body language that are impossible to fathom within the space of a short trip. Don't worry — just concentrate 101%.**

university museum, in a modern one-story structure nearby, exhibits contemporary Puerto Rican paintings and sculptures, along with archaeological evidence of the talents of the island's original Indian inhabitants.

More Indian relics, plus old Spanish coins and tiles, can be viewed in the **Ponce de León Museum** at **Caparra**, 4 miles (6½ km) west of San Juan on Route 2. Alongside this small white museum are the ruins of the house Ponce de León built and from which he directed the colonization of the island. In 1521, after a number of outbreaks of disease, the capital was moved to San Juan, and Caparra was abandoned. What's left of Ponce de León's house looks like ancient Roman ruins, earnestly preserved.

Cataño is an industrial area visible directly across the bay from the old city. Most of its buildings, though important to the economy of the island, spoil the view, but one is of rather more interest to visitors. The **Bacardi rum plant** offers an interesting and well-organized free guided tour. Small motorized trains carry visitors to the distilling and bottling plants. Free samples are dispensed, and in the gift shop you can buy bottles to take back home. For those more interested in history than in the production of rum, there is a fascinating museum that relates the story of the Bacardi family (who still own the business), from their arrival in Cuba from Spain, to their flight to Puerto Rico after the Cuban revolution in 1959, to their influence on the global drinks market.

San Juan's Resorts

Puerto Rico's popularity as a holiday island has risen enormously since the early 1960s. Most of the development and tourist infrastructure lies in a narrow strip along the coast, east of San Juan. **Condado** was the first; it had already been on the map with the jet set and saw further expansion when a string of high-rise hotels were built along the long stretches of sandy beach. Its main street, **Ashford Avenue**, has something of the Art-Deco feel of Miami's South Beach. As you stroll past the shops selling expensive top-drawer merchandise, you're likely to pass a number of impeccably dressed older women carrying impeccably coiffed toy poodles. As time has passed, the young energy has moved east, taking advantage of available land, and now **Isla Verde**, farther along the coast, has been developed—some say overdeveloped. This is where all the real action is. A number of large hotels with theaters, casinos, and restaurants attract high-rollers. Fast-food restaurants, bars, and gift shops fill the streets. The two main beaches of Isla Verde

Isla Verde's seaside stretch of attractions is peopled by legions of sun- and fun-seekers.

The Caribbean National Forest boasts countless species of flora and fauna.

are impressive (and they get very busy), but the resort is very close to the airport and can get a little noisy.

THE NORTHEAST

Heading east out of Isla Verde, it takes only a couple of minutes to leave the city behind. The coast road (Route 187) leads past the end of the runway at Muñoz Marín Airport on the left and Isla Verde's *balneario* (public beach) on the right. Travel over the little bridge that spans the entrance to Laguna la Torrecilla, and suddenly you are in the countryside.

The road runs along the coastline and through the **Bosque Estatal de Piñones**, an area of beautiful sandy beaches and coconut palms that until recently was a pristine environment where sleepy cattle sat under the trees. It is now a popular weekend picnic spot for city families, many of whom leave their litter behind when they depart. This sort of carelessness spoils Piñones (and many other beauty spots on the eastern coastline within easy reach of San Juan); an assemblage of broken bottles, leftover food, litter, and worse is something you can't fail to notice.

Head through Loíza, and on towards Río Grande. Here Route 187 meets Route 3, one of the major arterial roads around Puerto Rico; it's a very busy highway, so be aware and drive carefully. Take a left and proceed to Route 191; then turn right and head up toward **El Yunque** (the Anvil), 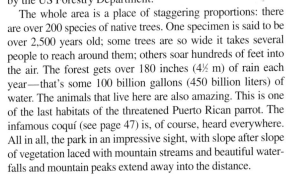 the most famous mountain in Puerto Rico. Normally capped with clouds it catches from the passing sea breezes, and sometimes entirely lost in a blanket of gray storm-clouds, the 3,496-ft (1,088-m) peak stands at the center of the **Caribbean National Forest**, an area of virgin rain forest preserved since 1876, when the island was still a Spanish colony. Originally a park of 12,300 acres (4,998 hectares), it now covers 28,000 acres (11,330 hectares) and is managed by the US Forestry Department.

The whole area is a place of staggering proportions: there are over 200 species of native trees. One specimen is said to be over 2,500 years old; some trees are so wide it takes several people to reach around them; others soar hundreds of feet into the air. The forest gets over 180 inches (4½ m) of rain each year—that's some 100 billion gallons (450 billion liters) of water. The animals that live here are also amazing. This is one of the last habitats of the threatened Puerto Rican parrot. The infamous coquí (see page 47) is, of course, heard everywhere. All in all, the park in an impressive sight, with slope after slope of vegetation laced with mountain streams and beautiful water-falls and mountain peaks extend away into the distance.

Cockfighting

Cockfighting is an immensely popular sport in Puerto Rico. You may be curious to see what happens during a contest—the crowd is often as interesting as the action in the ring. However, you should be aware that cockfighting is a very violent sport and is definitely not for everyone. To see a fight, visit the **Coliseo Gallístico** on route 37 in Isla Verde (Tel. 791-6005 for fight times).

Arriving via Route 191 you'll come right to the El Portal Tropical Forest Center at the entrance to the park. This facility presents important information about the history of the park, its plant and animal species, and its role in the local ecology. You can then travel on higher into the park, toward the summit. You can't drive the whole 8 miles (13 km) between the visitors center and the end of the road, but there are several car parks and rest areas on the way, so there's ample access. Two popular stops are **La Coca Falls**, on the right after the 5-mile (8-km) point, and the **Yokahú Observation Tower**, at the 5½-mile (9-km) point. Here you can photograph the surrounding slopes. The most spectacular cascade in the park, **La Mina Falls**, is just a 30-minute walk from the roadside, via Big Tree Trail.

Take a walk on any of the well-marked trails: the atmosphere is humid and the vegetation constantly damp (your best friends will be your insect repellent and your stout shoes), but the landscape is beautiful and fascinating.

El Yunque is included in many tours from San Juan; these usually include a trip to **Luquillo Beach**, which lies in the shadow of the peak, to the north. There is a popular balneario at Luquillo, which has restrooms, snack bars, and a children's play area. The beach is kept tidy and there is ample parking.

After Luquillo, Route 3 curves around toward the east coast of the island and to the town of **Fajardo**, which is a stepping-stone to the offshore islands of Vieques and Culebra. There is little to hold you in the town, except for a finger of land reach-

Balnearios

The Puerto Rican legislature created several *balnearios*, or public beaches, all around the island. For a small fee you can use the changing and restroom facilities, children's play area, and parking and picnic areas. They are also kept tidy—which is not always the case with other beaches.

Luquillo's balneario has sweeping vistas of empty coastline (and all the comforts of a well-maintained beach) to enjoy.

ing north out into the ocean. Take Route 997 to explore this area. On the way, you'll pass a large marina with fleets of charter boats and the El Conquistador Resort and Country Club with its golf course, marina, and private offshore island. At the very tip of the peninsula is Bahia la Cabezas and **Las Cabezas de San Juan Nature Reserve**, one of the newest reserves on the island. Acres of mangrove swamp cover the rocky outcrops, sheltering sandy beaches and providing a haven for herons and pelicans. You'll see hermit crabs scurrying across the ground, hiding in their shells as you approach. Faro de Fajardo (Fajardo lighthouse) stands amid all the greenery, protecting ships from the shallows to the north and east.

Isla de Vieques and Culebra

The islands of Vieques and Culebra, off of Puerto Rico's east coast, are a part of, yet in many ways totally separate from,

Culebra Island's mostly unsettled landscape is being protect-ed, which makes for lovely natural vistas such as this one.

the main island. The small populations here live a slower, more traditional life, and the headlong rush to get there yesterday, which you'll experience in some of the cities and towns of Puerto Rico, doesn't seem to exist here at all.

Vieques (pronounced *be-ay-kase*) is the largest of the two, though its name, from the Amerindian, means "small island." It's about 1½ hours by ferry from the coast, or a 30-minute flight from Isla Grande Airport in San Juan. An island of wonderful sandy beaches and farmland, it is also home to a large US military reserve. Regular military flights may mar the tranquillity somewhat, but they can't spoil the natural beauty. Much of the land has been leased back to farmers, and visitors can enjoy the wonderful beaches, although you'll need some form of photo ID to gain access to them. On the south coast you'll find **Sun Bay** and 3 miles (5 km) of fine government-run public beach (which was used as the location for the film *Lord of the Flies*). Nearby is **Mosquito Bay**, an appropriate name, since most of the island seems to have squadrons of the tiny winged beasts. This is a phosphorescent bay, and you can take a boat trip out into the water to agitate the microscopic organisms that give off the strange glow. It's a fascinating experience. The show is always better on a moonless night.

The capital of the island is **Isabel Segunda**, named in honor of the 19th-century Spanish Queen who was on the throne when work began on the fort, in the 1840s. Its shady plaza sees a constant stream of visitors, but no one rushes. There's little else to do but relax, and this is the real appeal of Vieques.

Culebra, much smaller at 21 sq miles (34 sq km), is north of Vieques. It is the largest rock in a collection of over twenty that attract sailors and divers from the main island. Culebra was known as the Spanish Virgin Island until the American takeover—it lies halfway between Puerto Rico and St. Thomas in the US Virgin Islands. Its only town is named **Dewey**, after Admiral George Dewey, a hero of the American-Spanish War of 1898. The local people are more apt to call it Pueblo.

Culebra is full of natural beauty: beaches (Flamenco is the most celebrated), clear waters full of marine life, and land awash with flowers. Most people come just to sit on the beach or walk in the fresh air. Much of the island is now managed

The Coquí

As the sun goes down, almost everywhere in Puerto Rico the air is filled with a "ko-kee, ko-kee, ko-kee," a sound heard nowhere else on earth. This is the call of a little frog named, not surprisingly, the coquí. Only a few centimeters long, these little creatures sing all night long to attract a mate. Only the males have a voice; the females are silent, spending their time listening intently for a "sexy" male!

by the US Fish and Wildlife Service, to preserve the environment. It makes an interesting day trip from Puerto Rico and a total contrast to hot days in the streets of Old San Juan.

THE SOUTHEAST

Traveling south from Fajardo you have the option of using Route 53 (a new toll road) or continuing on Route 3. Both roads lead past to the town of **Humacao**, and on toward the south coast. Just south of the Humacao is a left turn for **Palmas del Mar**, a growing resort area on the southeast coastline. A

Highlights of San Juan

Ballajá Barracks and the Museum of the Americas. *Tel. 724-5052.* Open Tue–Fri 10am–4pm, Sat and Sun 11am–5pm. Admission free.

Capilla del Cristo. *Calle Cristo*. Open Mon, Wed, and Fri 10:30am–3:30pm. Admission free.

Casa Blanca. *1 Calle San Sebastián; Tel. 724-5477.* Open Tue–Sat 9am–noon, 1–4:30pm. Admission: adults $1, children 50¢.

La Fortaleza. *Calle Recinto Oeste; Tel. 721-7000, ext. 2211/2323/2358* to reserve a spot on the tour. Open Mon–Fri 9am–4pm. Admission free. There is a smart casual dress code.

Fort San Cristóbal and El Morro. *Calle Norzagaray; Tel. 729-6960.* Open daily 9am–5pm. Admission: adults $2, children $1.

Pablo Casals Museum. *111 Calle San Sebastián; Tel. 723-9185.* Open Tue–Sat 9:30am–5pm. Admission: adults $1, children 50¢.

San Juan Cathedral. *153 Calle Cristo; Tel. 722-0861.* Open daily 8:30am–4pm, though may be closed during services. Admission free.

residential resort community built around wonderful stretches of beach, the resort offers numerous activities, including horse-back-riding, fishing, golf (two courses), and a casino.

East of the town of Yabucoa you'll find the start of the **Ruta Panoramica**. If you don't have time to follow this entire trail, at least drive along Route 3 south of Yabucoa to the area around the Cendro la Pandura peak. The road climbs via a series of switchback turns, and once at the top you'll have a clear view of the town lying in the flat plain below. The lifestyle of the people who live high on the hillside is fascinating. *Jíbaros* (country farmers) carry machetes to the fields, accompanied by their faithful hounds. Chickens scoot under cars as you approach. Around every turn, you'll marvel at how the houses can be built on such precipitous slopes. The road then leads along the southern coastal plain through several small towns to Playa de Ponce.

PONCE

Puerto Rico's second city, Ponce is as much steeped in history as Old San Juan. Founded in 1692, it was named after a relative of Juan Ponce de León, not the famous explorer himself. Ponce is a thriving port city, very modern in many ways,

Ponce's Our Lady of Guadalupe borders cool and beautiful Parque Degetau.

This bright and shiny vintage fire engine is housed in the even brighter Parque de Bombas building.

but it lives up to its name of "Pearl of the South." At the very heart of the city is a jewel of an old town, well-preserved thanks to a massive and expensive restoration program begun in the 1980s. Hundreds of careworn buildings were brought back to life, and power cables were buried underground and out of sight. Along with this physical transformation came a cultural change: Ponce has become a focus for social events that celebrate Puerto Rican history and tradition; several major festivals are held here throughout the year.

The focus of the city is **Parque Degetau** in Plaza Las Delicias (Delight Square), known by most locals as Plaza de Ponce. Most of what you want to see is within a few minutes' walk of this plaza, and cafés and restaurants for refreshments are also near at hand. You can spend a wonderful morning just soaking in the atmosphere. The park, with its shady trees, cooling fountains, and somber bronze statues, including one of Luis Muñoz Marín, is where people come to take a break from the midday heat. There's also a good ice-cream shop on the east side of the square.

At the heart of the square is the **Cathedral of our Lady of Guadalupe**, the city's main place of worship since the late 1600s. Steady streams of visitors step inside to light a candle. Behind the cathedral is perhaps the most famous building in the city, the **Parque de Bombas**. This small museum to the city's firefighters looks as though it were designed by a child and colored with crayons. Ornate wooden domes sitting atop four turrets that are painted in the brightest red and black stripes and highlighted with brilliant yellow. The structure was erected for a trade fair in 1882 and taken over by the *bomba* or firemen's organization. The displays detail the bravery of individuals who fought fires in the once mostly wooden old town.

> Music is always loud—delivery-truck drivers will even turn the volume higher when they leave their cabs so that they can hear their favorite songs while at their destination. You have to learn to enjoy it, because you won't escape it.

Casa Armstrong-Poventud (Armstrong-Poventud House) is the west side of the square. Once the family home of a Scottish-born banker and then later sold to the Poventud family, it's now a cultural center that holds various exhibitions throughout the year. The **Alcaldía** (city hall) is also interesting. Three American Presidents (the two Roosevelts and Herbert Hoover) delivered speeches from the balcony here. Built in 1840, it served as the town jail until 1905.

Radiating out from the main plaza are several roads, each of which with its own treasures. A number of the historic buildings have been converted to museums, but many are still residential or commercial buildings in daily use. Strolling along the streets you'll be able to admire the ornate Spanish colonial and neoclassical façades.

On Calle Isabel, east of the square, you'll find the **Ponce History Museum**. The building was actually two family houses—Casa Salazar and Casa Zapatar—that were joined to make room for this fascinating collection of archive material. The exhibits document the history of the town since its founding. Photographs bring to life the changes in lifestyle over the centuries. The comprehensive information plaques are in Spanish only, but there are guided tours in English every hour.

Behind the museum on Calle Cristina is the **La Perla Theater**. This was one of the first neoclassical structures to be built in the city, in 1864. Destroyed by an earthquake in the 1910s, it was rebuilt in 1940 and thoroughly restored as part of the major renovations of the late 1980s. It is once again at the center of the cultural activity for which Ponce is famed.

Another noteworthy museum on Calle Isabel is in Casa Serrallés: the **Museum of Puerto Rican Music** traces the complicated development of the island's distinctive musical legacy, from Amerindian influences to the blending of Spanish colonial musical styles.

One of the homes that has only recently opened its doors to visitors is **Casa Wiechers Villaronga** on Calle Reina. Designed in 1911 by Alfredo Wiechers for the Villaronga-Mercado family, it is full of elegant Art-Deco features.

Ponce is a lively town, and street vendors can be found on every corner. The town **market** at Calle Atocha, one block from the main square, operates as it has done for generations. Here you'll find fresh vegetables and fruit galore.

Ponce also has some surprises outside the historic quarter. On El Vigía Hill, above the town to the north, are two interesting attractions. One is a 100-ft (30½-m) high cross that overlooks the city. Known locally as **Cruz del Vigía**, it was built in 1984; this concrete cross replaced a wooden one from the last century. There is an observation area at the point at which the arms spread; from here you can get a panoramic view over Ponce and out toward the coast.

Set just below Cruz del Vigía, one of the finest houses in Ponce, **Castillo Serrallés** (Serrallés Castle) is not a castle but actually a spectacular family home built in the 1930s for the

Graceful figures stand in the Italian School gallery at the Museo de Arte de Ponce.

Serrallés family, owners of the Don Q rum company. With its red-tiled roof and pastel pink exterior, the structure is a lovely example of the Spanish Revival style. It is full of beautiful furniture owned by various family members. The gardens have been designed in formal French style, with lots of carefully trimmed box hedges and expansive lawns; from here you can look down on Ponce town. Since 1986 the house has been owned by the Ponce Municipal Government, which now operates it as a museum and meeting center.

South of the historic town center, on Avenue of the Americas (a modern two-lane highway) is the **Museo de Arte de Ponce** (Ponce Art Museum). This collection of European and Puerto Rican art, probably the finest in the Caribbean, would be very much at home in any European capital. The museum is the brainchild of Luis Ferré, industrialist and onetime governor of Puerto Rico, who has put great effort into bringing works of art to the town. More than 1,600 paintings and sculptures make up the collection, which covers five centuries of western art. The Flemish collection features work by Paul Bril (1554–1626) and David Teniers (1610–1690). The Spanish collection has a piece by El Greco (1541–1614). Nicholas Maes (1632–1693) is represented in the Dutch collection, and British artists include Joshua Reynolds (1723–1792), Thomas Gainsborough (1727–1788) and George Romney (1734–1802). Pride of place is taken by the painting *Flaming June*, by Frederick Lord Leighton (1830–1896). The gallery offers a guided tour in English every afternoon at 2pm.

The city of Ponce actually sits some 3 miles (5 km) inland, but the local residents take every opportunity to go to the coast.

Puerto Rican Coffee— Some of the Finest in the World!

Coffee plants were introduced to the island in 1736 and they immediately flourished on the humid slopes of the interior mountain. Coffee is still one of the most popular non-alcoholic drinks on the island. There are many grades of coffee in the world, but only three are classed as **Café Superior Premium** (the highest grade): Blue Mountain from Jamaica, Kona from Hawaii, and **Alto Grande** from Puerto Rico. The beans produce a cup of joe that is full-flavored but not too strong. Even the Vatican agreed—it was the only coffee served to popes for many years.

The city beach is kept passably tidy by litter patrols. One spot where you're bound to meet the locals is **La Guancha**, a boardwalk area between the beach, Ponce Marina, and the commercial docks. It's a great place for strolling and gazing out over the water. There's a tower to climb if you want a bird's-eye view. Numerous kiosks sell cold beer and Puerto Rican snacks. The area's always buzzing at weekends.

While at La Guancha you may see groups of people across the narrow bay staring down into the water. More likely than not, they're trying to catch sight of the giant tarpon that have taken to swimming around in the shallows. Hundreds of these fish—some are up to 7 ft (2 m) long—congregate here because they've learned they'll be well supplied with tasty tidbits offered by the humans on shore.

North of Ponce are attractions of a different kind. Take Route 503 out of town—this road runs along the banks of the Río Portuguéz—and after about a mile and a half (2 km) you'll arrive at the **Tibes Indian Ceremonial Park**, one of the most important Amerindian archaeological sites in the Caribbean. The ceremonial site and cemetery are across the river, and you may not enter without a guide. A small museum explains the known history of the Amerindian races; it has a number of cabinets holding artifacts, as well as a skeleton, still in the traditional fetal burial position. Once you're into the park, the ceremonial grounds come into view. Open spaces discovered since the 1960s are now believed to be used for "ball games," which had an important though as yet only poorly understood ceremonial purpose in Indian culture.

High in the hills behind Ponce is **Hacienda Buena Vista**. To get there, take Route 10, a major north-south artery. The road climbs steeply into dense vegetation and cooler air before you see signs for the hacienda; the climate and environmental conditions here were ideal for the coffee that the plantation

These replicas of Taíno grass homes at Tibes Indian Ceremonial Park are based on archaeological study of the site.

began to grow more than 150 years ago. The plantation fell into neglect in the 20th century, but since 1984 it has been returned to its original state by The Conservation Trust of Puerto Rico. Agricultural machinery such as coffee bean huskers can be seen in the original buildings, and the water mill and canals, which harnessed the power of the Canas River, are now in working order. The facility shows how plantations used to operate and offer a fascinating insight into agricultural life in Puerto Rico all those years ago. Advance reservations are required for the tours (see page 64).

THE SOUTHWEST

West of Ponce there are a number of *bosques estatales* (state forests) and acres of farmland with grazing cattle and commercial stables. Rainfall is much lighter here than in the east, and the forests are more temperate than tropical.

Bosque Estatal de Guánica (Guánica State Forest), on the south coast thirty minutes from Ponce, is one of the largest tracts of tropical dry forest in the world. The fascinating rocky landscape is home to thousands of cacti and other desert plants (over 700 species all together). Named a World Biosphere Reserve, the area includes several sandy beaches. To see the park at its best, though, take the inland route (Route 334) rather than the coast road. There is too much evidence of human activity on the beaches; the litter and burned-out cars spoil some of the beautiful views.

Further east along Route 116 you'll reach **La Parguera**, a small town on the south coast surrounded by thousands of acres of mangroves. A pretty town with a seaside atmosphere, it is a popular vacation spot for city-dwelling Puerto Ricans. One of the most enticing activities in La Parguera is exploring the mangroves (some of the tunnels are hundreds of yards deep) and the small offshore islands where you can picnic, swim, and snorkel all day. The waters offshore are full of sealife and wonderfully clear. (Rental boats are available.)

Just east of La Parguera is **Phosphorescent Bay**, known for its glowing water filled with micro-organisms. Over the years many residents have built houseboats on the margins of the mangrove, and this has caused problems for the sensitive environment of the bay. The situation is said to be improving now, as new environmental controls are being put into place.

Heading west beyond La Parguera, you'll need to use secondary roads, but these are in surprisingly good condition and relatively quiet. It's almost a *pampas* landscape here, with grassy slopes and horses galore. **Boquerón**, a small village on the west coast, has arguably the most beautiful *balneario* (public beach) on Puerto Rico, a long arc of fine sand backed by sea grapes and palm trees. The settlement is growing due to its popularity, and a new marina is taking shape,

The still-working Faro de Cabo Rojo is perched on sheer cliffs that make for a breathtaking visit.

but it still retains the feel of its origins as a fishing village. When the catches arrive, small temporary stalls are set up around the tiny town square. You can buy fresh clams and oysters, which can be shucked for you to eat as you go. There are a few small hotels here, which soon fill up on weekends and holidays, but if you arrive midweek or out of season, you may find that you are the only visitors.

South of Boquerón you leave the world behind. Make your way along Route 301 towards **Cabo Rojo** and the lighthouse at the southwest tip of the island to really enjoy natural Puerto Rico. Fishing is the main way people make a living here—between mangrove outcrops are many small shacks with boats tied up to rickety wooden jetties. The salt flats that you see are still harvested commercially. Eventually, the tar-

mac stops and the road changes to a simple dirt track. The surface is reasonable, so don't worry about continuing on. You'll travel over a narrow bridge and enter a section of the **Bosque Estatal de Boquerón**. Leave you car below the lighthouse and walk up the hill to reach it (a five-minute walk for the reasonably fit). Turn around as you climb the hill, and a wonderful sandy bay will open out in front of you. Pelicans play and feed, and frigate birds wheel in the sky above.

The **Faro de Cabo Rojo** (Cabo Rojo Lighthouse) has been sadly neglected, but the light still plays an important part in protecting shipping off the island. It sits atop some of the highest cliffs on Puerto Rico, a truly spectacular sight. But beware of going too close to the edge, as there are no fences here.

Inland from La Parguera and Boquerón is pretty **San Germán**, once also set on the coast but moved inland after the original site was sacked several times. Built on an undulating hillside, the town is the epitome of the Spanish colonial style. Its two town squares have not yet been spoiled by neon fast-food signs. There's much of architectural interest around the pretty promenades and grand houses. Over 200 named buildings are under protection, but unfortunately, as yet, there is no tourist information office in the town, and many of the buildings are neither identified nor open to the public. Just enjoy the beautiful views and stroll along the streets to take in all the detail.

The major building of importance here is the **Iglesia Porta Coeli** (Church of the Gate of Heaven), a tiny terra-cotta chapel and convent founded in 1606. It sits in the lower of two squares in the town. The heart of one of the most important religious communities on the island in its early years, it was later used as a schoolhouse and poorhouse before being handed over to the government in 1949. After renovations in 1960, it was opened to the public. The new complex includes the **Museo de Arte Religioso** (Museum of Religious Art), which features a collection of Puerto Rican *santos*, carved religious figures and icons.

North of Boquerón is the city of **Mayagüez**, the major urban center of the west coast and the end of the Ruta Panoramica. The old city was destroyed in an earthquake in 1918; as a result, Mayagüez is less interesting in terms of architecture than other settlements. It is, however, a popular base from which to explore the west coast (there are frequent direct flights between Mayagüez and San Juan). A number of large international hotels offer a good standard of accommodation and facilities such as golf and casinos.

The University of Puerto Rico's campus at Mayagüez has an internationally recognized **Tropical Agriculture Research Center**, which, among other activities, cultivates several hundred tropical species. The center is open to the public, but since it has no refreshment facilities or play areas for children, it's for dedicated gardeners only.

Fifty miles (80 km) off the coast is **Mona Island**, called "the Galapagos of Puerto Rico." This isolated place, characterized by a coastline of high cliffs, is home to turtles, iguanas, and endangered pelicans. There is no human settlement today, but there is evidence that Taíno Indians once lived here. Columbus is also said to have landed, as did Ponce de León. Camping trips of the "commune-with nature" variety can be arranged from Mayagüez.

THE NORTHWEST

The northwest of Puerto Rico is the surfing capital of the Antilles, with great waves rising offshore. In-

The Iglesia Porta Coeli has, in its time, hosted the devout, the young, and the broke.

land is some of the most beautiful and undeveloped karst landscape anywhere. The region produces most of the Puerto Rican coffee crop, once the only coffee drunk in the Vatican.

Once north of Mayagüez, head west on Route 115 to **Rincón**. This small town and low-key resort is the surfing center for all the beaches along the coast. North from town is **Punta Higuaro**, one of the most popular beaches, and the **Faro de Rincón** (Rincón Lighthouse). This warning tower, which is surrounded by a neat park area with a café and gift shop, makes an ideal platform for whale-watching. Groups of the leviathans pass here on their migrations. Telescopes allow

Swim, surf, or simply enjoy the sunset at Aguadilla's beautiful beaches.

you to scan the horizon for their watery exhalations.

Farther north along the coast, just south of the small town of **Aguada**, is a monument commemorating the landing of Cristóbal Colón on the island in 1493. Though no one is really sure of the precise landing site (Columbus is renowned for having been less than accurate in documenting his landing sites), the small park with its column and naïve paintings depicting Spanish colonization serves its purpose well.

North of the town of **Aguadilla**, traveling out toward the airport and Rafael Hernandez air force base, are a series of fine bathing and surfing beaches. The most famous is **Crash Boat Beach**, named after a shipwreck that happened just offshore. The beach is always busy, but the most exciting stretch is the northern section, where the fishing boats rest. Most hours of the morning there are ships coming ashore with their meager, but extremely fresh, catch. The boats are brightly colored and carefully tended to ensure that they are always in peak condition—not one is splintered or sun-bleached.

Traveling back along the northern coast there is little to draw the eye. Inland however, it's a different story. South of the busy town of **Arecibo** are a number of attractions that would make a fine day-trip from San Juan (none is more than a 90-minute drive from the capital).

Route 129 from Arecibo leads to one of the most important and mysterious scientific instruments in the world. **Arecibo Observatory** has the largest single-dish radio telescope in the world; 1,000 ft (305 m) in diameter, it has been silently scanning the universe, making maps of distant solar systems, and listening for messages from other planets since 1960. The Observatory is part of Cornell University's National Astronomy and Ionosphere Center; it operates 24 hours a day. The center likes to emphasize the serious scientific work it undertakes— such as detecting extremely weak radio pulses from the very corners of the known universe, which take 100 million years to reach the earth. Some visitors are more impressed by the fact that the observatory was used for location shots in the James Bond film *Goldeneye* and, more recently, in *Contact*, starring Jodie Foster. A viewing platform allows you to look down on the massive dish, and in the education center, opened in 1997, visitors can undertake simple and safe experiments to learn more about physics and the solar system.

The Observatory sits in the heart of karst country, a region of archetypal limestone erosion. Wave upon wave of small smooth hillocks known as "haystacks" cover the land, and the roads bend and weave around these forested mounds and through small villages nestled in the valleys. The name "karst" is taken from a region of Yugoslavia that has these same geographical characteristics. One striking feature of all karst landscapes is that the erosion of the limestone layers by rainwater creates cave systems, where weaker rock is worn away from under stronger rock that remains intact. Puerto Rico has one of the most dramatic cave systems yet discovered, in an area known as **Parque de las Cavernas del Río Camuy** (Río

Highlights Around the Island

Arecibo Observatory, Arecibo. *Route 625; Tel. 878-2612*. Open Wed–Fri noon–4pm, Sat and Sun 9am–4pm. Admission: adults $3.50, children $1.50.

Caguana Indian Ceremonial Park. *Route 111, Kilometer 12.3; Tel. 894-7325*. Open daily 9am–4:30pm. Admission free.

Hacienda Buena Vista, Ponce. *Route 10, Kilometer 16.8; Tel. 772-5882 for reservations*. Open Fri–Sun. Reservations required; tours in English at 1:30. Admission: adults $5, children $2.

Iglesia Porta Coeli, San Germán. *Route 102; Tel. 892-5845*. Open Wed–Sun 9am–4:45pm. Admission free.

Parque de Bombas, Ponce. *Plaza Las Delicias*. Open Mon–Fri 9:30am–6pm. Admission free.

Ponce Art Museum, Ponce. *Avenida Las Américas; Tel. 848-0505*. Open daily 10am–5pm. Admission: adults $4, children $2.

Río Camuy Cave Park. *Route 129, Kilometer 18.9; Tel. 898-3100*. Open Tue–Sun 8am–5pm (last tour departs 3:50). Admission: adults $10, children $7.

Serrallés Castle, Ponce. *17 El Vigía Hill; Tel. 259-1774*. Open Tue–Thur 9:30am–5pm, Fri–Sun 9:30am–5:30pm. Admission: adults $3, children $1.50.

Tibes Indian Ceremonial Park, Ponce. *Route 503, Kilometer 2.7; Tel. 840-2255*. Open Tue–Sun 9am–4pm. Admission: adults $2; children $1.

El Yunque Visitors Center. *Caribbean National Forest, Route 191; Tel. 888-1880*. Mon–Fri 7:30am–5pm, Sat and Sun 8am–5pm. Admission: adults $3, children $1.50.

Camuy Cave Park), a little way south of the Observatory, just off Route 129. Tourist trains carry passengers between the caves and sinkholes (deep vertical shafts created when cave roofs collapse) that make up the park. A long video (Spanish only) shows what to expect before you set out. The giant **Cueva Clara** (Clara Cave) is reached by descending into a sinkhole; once in its depths, a narrow entrance leads to a cavern of cathedral-like dimensions—it is said the largest section of the cave could hold the El Morro fort. The caves and sinkholes have taken millions of years to erode; many of the stalagmites and stalactites have

The Arecibo Observatory uses its resources by searching for new data and for first contact.

been hundreds of thousands of years in formation. An underground river, the Río Camuy, is responsible for much of the work. It still flows today, enlarging its path through the rock.

The whole cave park is a truly awesome sight, with holes 300 ft (91 m) deep and 200 ft (61 m) across, and caves thousands of feet deep, all surrounded by pristine forest. Some say that the fountain of youth is here, in the clean water filtering through the limestone from the surface. You don't have to believe the legends, but taste the water anyway—it's very sweet, and it can't hurt to wish just a little.

From the caves it's a short drive to **Lares**, the island's center of coffee production. The sweet brew made from Puerto Rican beans is considered one of the finest in the world, though production is small. Coffee plants, usually interspersed with other crops such as bananas or plantains, can be seen growing on the high hillsides; it is a crop that enjoys good drainage and lots of humidity, which the large banana leaves help to conserve.

From Lares take Route 111 to reach the most important Amerindian site on Puerto Rico, the **Parque Ceremonial**

Ruta Panoramica and the Interior

The **Ruta Panoramica** (Panoramic Route) allows visitors to travel along small country roads to see the most unspoiled parts of Puerto Rico's interior. It takes a route along the "backbone" of the island, across the wide sierras and over the central mountain range, the **Cordillera Central**. The road passes the highest point—**Cerro de Punta**, at 4,390 ft (1,338 m)—and several mountain forest reserves, such as Reserve Forestal Maricao in the east. All have picnic tables and panoramic viewing points.

But it isn't only the Ruta Panoramica that allows you to escape modern Puerto Rico for a while. Almost any route in the interior will lead to a quiet natural forest. El Yunque is the most popular and well known natural area, but places such as the **Reserve Forestal Carite** (Guavate Forest) south of San Juan, or the **Bosque Estatal de Guajataca** in the northeast can provide private places for walking and hiking.

The interior of Puerto Rico also has a number of lakes for boating or fishing. The **Embalse Río Grande de Loíza** is the nearest to the city, just south of the suburbs. And **Lago de Guajataca**, southeast of Arecibo, is popular on the weekends, when pig roasts are the order of the day at roadside restaurants.

A tour through the Río Camuny caves promises to be a quite otherworldly experience.

Indígena Caguana (Caguana Indian Ceremonial Park). The park is set in a wide valley surrounded by limestone peaks, one of which is said to represent the supreme god of the Taínos. The several ceremonial ball courts discovered and excavated here suggest the site was one of the Indians' major centers of worship. The Taínos were still living happily on the island when Columbus arrived in 1493; archaeological finds here date back to 1200 B.C. The ball courts, edged with stones—some with symbols carved on them—are set in fine gardens planted with many native tree species. A small museum displays pottery and other artifacts found at the site.

From Arecibo on the coast, it's an hour along the fast Route 22 toll road to San Juan. Many of the villages and towns along the way are small industrial outposts for the suburbs of

These stone petroglyphs carved by the Taíno line their ceremonial ball parks.

Cataño. Just before reaching the city, however, is a resort that is developing into an important provider of visitor accommodations. **Dorado** has several large resort hotels, all of which occupy private grounds near the pretty sandy beaches. These are self-contained hotels, with facilities such as golf courses and night-time entertainment. There is however, little tourist infrastructure in the immediate vicinity. The town of Dorado, with restaurants and shops, is 2½ miles (4 km) from the nearest hotel along the strip. The Dorado resort area began life as a large plantation, owned by the Livingston family; the first hotel built here—the Hyatt Dorado Beach Hotel—incorporated the old plantation house into its original design.

EXCURSION TO St. THOMAS

The shopping mecca of the Caribbean, St. Thomas is the most densely populated of the three US Virgin Islands (the others are St. John and St. Croix). Easily reached from San Juan—just a 40-minute flight from Muñoz Marín International Airport—St. Thomas has become a "must-visit" island for many people. It's a duty-free haven, where luxury goods can be 40% cheaper than at home. This is particularly advantageous to US citizens, who can claim an allowance of $1,200 per person, regardless of age. Many Puerto Ricans hop across for the day, to take advantage of the bargains. During the flight over from San Juan, you'll be able to get a bird's-eye view of most of the neighboring US and British Virgin Islands.

Charlotte Amalie

The capital of St. Thomas, **Charlotte Amalie** (pronounced "amahlia"), sits on one of the finest natural harbors in the world. Named by Danish settlers after the wife of King Christian V, the settlement started out as a trading port (a tradition that continues with great success today). The downtown area, resting between the surrounding hills and the harbor, is a warren of old streets and red roofs best seen from above. One lasting legacy of the Danish colonization is the street names.

Warehouses built along the harbor by 17th- and 18th-century Danish merchants still play host to hundreds of traders. But now, instead of stocking such staples as cotton, flour, or salt, the stores are filled with the modern version of "pirate booty" — gold, gems, watches, and designer goods. The main shopping streets lie close to the waterfront. A series of narrow alleys are filled with craft, clothing, and jewelry shops, along with cafés and restaurants that provide welcome relief once you've become "shopped out."

But Charlotte Amalie is not just a shopper's paradise. There are historic gems to be discovered here as well. Perhaps the most prominent is **Fort Christian**, which sits to the east of downtown. Work on the fort began in 1671, to protect the harbor. The terra-cotta walls, pretty painted shutters, and crenellated clock tower give the building a cozy rather than a fearsome look. The interior has been transformed into a museum of life in the US Virgin Islands: colonial furniture, archive documents, and old photographs of the islands, people, and towns. Take a walk onto the walls of the fort for a wonderful view over the seafront and the colorful Vendors Plaza, a craft market under bright parasols that has a permanent home in the fort's shadow.

Next to the fort is the pretty **Legislature building** with a classical façade painted bright lime green. Finished in 1874, the building was originally used as a barracks for troops based at the fort. Behind the fort and the Vendors Plaza is **Emancipation Park**, perhaps the one place in town where you can sit in the shade of the trees and enjoy the cooling sea breeze after your sightseeing and shopping. The park was named to commemorate the freeing of the slaves in 1848. Across Tolbod Gade is the Tourist Information Office, where you can pick up maps and other information. On the northern corner of Tolbod Gade is the main post office. Make your way in that direction, but don't be tempted to turn right and head for the stores just yet. Take the steps to **Kongens Gade**, which is the street behind the Lutheran Church. The steps climb onto the steep hill that has many of the oldest and most important buildings of Danish Charlotte Amalie. The family houses of the merchants and civil servants where built high on this rise—named **Government Hill**—to take advantage of the cooling breeze. Kongens Gade itself has several buildings dating back to the late 18th and early 19th centuries. Hotel 1829, named for the year in which it was built, sits amid other fine homes. Walk past Hotel 1829 and pause at the steps beside it, which climb higher onto Government Hill. These are the **99 Steps**, one of a series built by the Danes in the mid 1700s to allow pedestrian access to the town below. The 99 Steps are the longest in town, but whoever named the flight must have become tired toward the end and miscounted—there are in fact 103.

Before climbing the steps, make a small detour farther along Kongens Gade, past the Lutheran Parsonage (1725), to reach **Government House**, an archetypal colonial mansion. Now the office for the Governor of the USVIs, this 1867 structure was originally used for meetings of the Danish Colonial Council; it was totally renovated in 1974. Nearby is **Seven Arches House Museum**, once the home of a Danish master craftsman. The house has a "welcoming arms" staircase—fashionable in the 18th century—leading to the entrance. Renovated and filled with period furniture, walking through it is a step back in time.

Retrace your route to the 99 Steps and climb to the summit of Government Hill. At the top, just when you may feel in need of a rest, you'll find **Haagensen House**, another renovated period property. Its original owner, Hans Haagensen, was a Danish banker. Those who don't want to climb the steps can take a shuttle to Haagensen House from the Pampered Pirate gift shop on Norre Gade. The remains of **Blackbeard's Castle**—said to be the home of the famous pirate, whose real name was Edward Teach—can also be seen here.

Fort Christian in Charlotte Amalie now houses many artifacts of the lives it was once built to protect.

Perhaps one of the most beautiful and unusual buildings in Charlotte Amalie is the **St. Thomas Synagogue**, on Crystal Gade. This is the oldest synagogue building in continual use under the American flag. The Jewish congregation has always been strong here, from the very earliest days of Danish settlement in 1655. When the all-consuming fire of 1831 broke out, 64 families were worshipping in the small synagogue. Only one scroll could be saved before the flames destroyed the building. The present structure was built on the same spot and opened in 1833. The synagogue has sand on the floor, symbolic of the Jewish flight from Egypt.

The **cruise port** is situated at the West Indian Company Dock, a mile or so east of town. The thirty-minute walk around the harbor is pleasant if the traffic is not too busy. Those who want to ride will find numerous taxis waiting to take them to and from Charlotte Amalie. The dock is one of the largest, and busiest, in the Caribbean. Old Danish warehouses along the dockside have been transformed in recent years, creating **Havensight Shopping Mall**. Over 80 tax-free boutiques with cafés and restaurants sit only feet away from the huge ships. You will also find the ticket office for **Atlantis Submarine** in the Havensight Mall. This mini-submarine, which seats around thirty, takes you some 60 ft (18 m) under the sea to view coral reefs and the marine life that inhabits them. A ferry takes you out to Buck Island some 3 miles (5 km) offshore to rendezvous with the sub, which then submerges to spend about an hour exploring the reef around the island. Shoals of yellow-tailed snapper surround the machine, along with sharks, rays, and turtles. It is great fun for young and old alike and a safe way to see the underwater world.

Beside the cruise port is **Flag Hill**, rising 700 ft (214 m) above sea level. From here you can enjoy the panoramic

The relatively Danish character of Charlotte Amalie offers a different feel than its close neighbor, Puerto Rico.

views over Charlotte Amalie, the surrounding hills, and the harbor. Paradise Point Tramway has been built to carry passengers to a platform, which is ideal for photographers. The seven-minute journey to the top gives a clear view of Havensight and the cruise port and there are is a café/bar in case you want to stop for refreshment.

Around the Island

Like most of the Virgin Islands, St. Thomas is full of hills. The roads twist and turn around sharp bends and roll up and over undulations. To see the main attractions of St. Thomas it's best to head directly north up into the hills; you'll be able to enjoy the beautiful views back towards Charlotte Amalie along the way. **Drake's Seat**, thought to

This view of Magens Bay is the main draw to Mountain Top —though for some, it may be their banana daiquiris.

mark the spot where Francis Drake sat and watched ships moving to and from San Juan, offers breathtaking views of the northern coastline and **Magens Bay**, the site of what is probably the best beach on St. Thomas, and one of the most famous in the Caribbean. **Estate St. Peter Greathouse and Botanical Gardens** takes up 11 acres (4½ hectares) along the ridge top near the summit of St. Peter peak. The estate was established in the 1800s and was owned in the 1930s by Virgin Islands Governor Lawrence Cramer. Both the house and the gardens were totally destroyed by Hurricane Hugo in 1989. Today they are back to their beautiful best, and the house has been restored to combine history with modern amenities. The observation deck around the house is the perfect perch from which to admire the view. If you're feeling more energetic, follow the nature trail through the garden.

At nearby **Mountain Top**—1,547 ft (472 m) above the bay, and higher than Drake's Seat—you'll find a sophisticated shopping mall and large bar area with almost non-stop daiquiris (they claim to have invented the banana daiquiri here). Everyone comes with a camera, so you may have to wait a while to get a shot of the view.

Magens Bay is a beautiful stretch of sand with a slight kink in the center, which gives it the epithet "heart-shaped." Because it is so sheltered, it's a safe place for children to swim and for everyone to snorkel, though it can get very busy. In the rolling hillside behind the beach is **Mahogany Run Golf Course**, so you could have a round in the morning and swim and snorkel in the afternoon.

On the eastern end of the island, amid a number of large hotel complexes, is **Coki Point**, a pleasant beach. At the end of the point is **Coral World**, which offers a fascinating look at life under the water. The attraction centers around a number of different controlled marine environments, each with its own animals or fish. Watch out for the sting-ray, shark, and turtle pools, where regular feeding times are posted; you'll even get a chance to pet some of the exhibits. Pride of place at Coral World must go to the genuine coral reef, which has been implanted in the open water offshore. An underground viewing area reached via a walkway allows you to observe the daily activity of the reef fish and some of the larger wild creatures who swim in for the free food provided by Coral World staff.

Coki Beach is popular spot for snorkelers, simply because there is so much sea-life here, thanks to the regular feedings provided by Coral World around their reef. Many of the cruise ships bus their passengers in here for snorkeling so it can get busy, but you are almost always guaranteed a good show of marine life.

WHAT TO DO

SHOPPING

There's nothing more fun after a day of culture and history than to indulge in a little shopping, and one of the great things about old San Juan is that the shops and the history intertwine. Many shops are housed in distinguished buildings in the heart of the old town. Old San Juan is an ideal place for browsing and comparison shopping—its small arcades and streets are full of the familiar as well as the strange and exotic. Local handicrafts reflect a mix of traditional Spanish and African techniques and styles. Children will easily be able to find something to buy with their few dollars pocket money, and, if your budget allows, you can spend thousands on a unique piece of art or sculpture. You will also find that many well-known brand names of popular items may be less expensive here than at home.

What to Buy

Here are some items to look for while exploring the island:

Antiques. The many interesting antiques shops here vouch for the authenticity of old Spanish and Puerto Rican furniture, clocks, and bric-a-brac.

Art. The art scene is flourishing in Puerto Rico. Many of the galleries in San Juan exhibit the work of up-and-coming Latin American artists; some of the best galleries and shops are to be found on Calle Cruz, Calle Cristo, and Calle San José. You'll find work in all media—oils, pastels, and gouache, as well as sculptures. Haitian pieces are also available in some of the galleries of Old San Juan.

Bamboo. Flutes, whistles, and other novelties carved from this locally grown hollow-stemmed plant are available in crafts stores throughout the island.

Children's clothing. Very stylish togs for tots, including fancy wear from Spain, are available here.

Cigars. Locally grown tobacco is used in hand-rolled cigars (you can watch cigar-makers at work in various places in San Juan). Though more expensive than Dominican—the harvest here is small—Puerto Rican cigars are said to be mild and full of flavor.

Designer goods. You can find the real thing in trendy shops and boutiques, or scour the markets for knock-offs of designer watches, bags, and clothing.

Evil-eye charms. Amulets and other trinkets, many hand-carved, are reminders of the African strain in Puerto Rican culture.

Fanciful carnival masks and other native art can make for unique souvenirs.

Fabrics. Hand-printed textiles in novel designs are a growing industry on the island.

Guayaberas. The best-dressed Puerto Rican gentlemen wear these tailored, embroidered shirts for many occasions.

Hammocks. The old Indian industry is still alive here. Hammocks come in a remarkable variety of styles, colors, and sizes (a miniature model for your cat, a double-wide hammock for the adventurous).

Cigar-lovers should definitely stop by one of the local outlets; Puerto Rican tobacco makes for a great smoke.

Imported goods. Window-shopping reveals surprises galore: Swiss watches, Indian saris, Balinese sarongs, German crystal, and more.

Jewelry. From basic materials such as shells and beads to chic expensive rings and brooches of gold and precious stones.

Kites. Buy them, then fly them; you won't need to wait until you return home to enjoy this purchase.

Lace. A once dying art is being revived in mountain villages in the west. It's pretty, but extremely pricey.

Macramé. A booming cottage industry. Popular items made from knotted threads or cords include framed "scenes" or useful objects like coasters.

Musical instruments. Puerto-Rican style marimbas, xylophones, or other instruments make interesting and sometimes inexpensive souvenirs. Some are made from dried gourd or calabash. Some are filled with seeds for shaking (*maracas*), others notched on the outside for rhythmical scraping (*güiro*).

Naïve Amerindian images. Stone carvings of bats, turtles, and monkeys transformed onto T-shirts or wall prints.

Outlet goods. Some of the best known names in retailing have shops in the old town, where you're sure to find a bargain.

Pavas. Straw hats worn by every *jíbaro*.

Rum. Puerto Rican brands of rum—light, dark, and aged—are best-sellers. **Don Q** is the best-known Puerto Rican brand (named after Don Quixote, a hero of the distillery's founder), but **Bacardi** now calls Puerto Rico home (after leaving Cuba at the time of the revolution) and is by far the biggest producer. Other labels to try are Barrilito, Palo Viejo, and Ron Rico. Prices are much cheaper in duty-free St. Thomas, if you're planning a side trip.

Santos. These hand-carved statuettes of saints or religious scenes are eminently portable. You'll be able to choose from the naïve to the sophisticated.

Voodoo dolls and masks. Serious or whimsical, grotesque or just exotic. You may have a chance to see some used in a fiesta parade.

Wooden bowls and plates. Most of these items are fashioned from native trees.

Zoological figurines. Turtles, elephants, giraffes, and, most prevalent, images of Puerto Rico's beloved tree frog, the coquí.

ENTERTAINMENT
Music

Music is the ingredient that keeps this island moving, and, whatever their age, Puerto Ricans cannot help but dance to any beat they hear. The popular rhythms are a unique mixture of Spanish and African influences, though the instruments traditionally used have antecedents going back further than the Spanish colonial and African slave imports. The güiro, a percussion instrument made of a notched dried gourd, was developed by the Taíno Indians. To this the Spanish added several types of guitars, with the ten-stringed cuatro being the most famous—it is the national instrument of Puerto Rico. African slaves brought with them the wherewithal to produce tambours, wood covered in animal skin to create drums, and maracas, dried

San Juan at night is a place full of electricity and definitely worth exploring.

gourds filled with seeds. These instruments played together form the basic "orchestra" for several popular musical genres.

Puerto Rican **folk music** is rich with songs based on real-life issues faced by the *jíbaros,* the ordinary country folk of the island—death, unrequited love, and poverty resulting from bad harvests. **Salsa** is probably the most famous form of music

Dancers perform to the strains of Puerto Rican folk music, jíbaro songs that tell of the good times and the bad.

to emerge from Puerto Rico. Ironically, salsa (which means "sauce") was imported back to the island from the Puerto Rican community who settled in New York city in the late 1940s. Salsa combines an array of percussion instruments with a swinging horn section. You will hear it everywhere. A much older "Latin" dance making a comeback is the **merengue**, which, when it first became popular, was considered to be so provocative that it was banned by the Spanish authorities.

Finally, there are the compelling *bomba* and the *plena*. A genre directly related to the rhythmic beats of African music, bomba makes use of animal-skin drums along with maracas and higher pitched percussion instruments. Plena music is said to have its roots in Spanish colonial courtly behavior, though the instruments used are also Taíno and African. Most of the stage shows at the larger hotels features these two types of music.

Theater

Teatro Tapia (Tel. 721-0169) in Old San Juan and the **Centro de Bellas Artes** (Tel. 725-7337) in the suburb of Santurce hold regular performances that range from traditional ballet to classical theater to modern works by today's most prodigious talents. **Teatro La Perla** (Tel. 843-4080) in Ponce also has a full card of performances, especially at festival time.

Casals Festival

The highlight of the annual cultural calendar is the *Festival Casals,* a month full of performances given by the world's great concert artists. Originally inspired by the peerless Spanish cellist and conductor Pablo Casals, who spent his last years in Puerto Rico, the festival attracts thousands of music lovers. It takes place every June on the campus of the University of Puerto Rico at Río Piedras.

A day at the Races?

The **El Comandante** horse-racing track (Tel. 724-6060), to the southeast of San Juan on route 3, hosts five race meetings each week. The sport is very popular with Puerto Ricans and the gambling is fast and furious.

Puerto Rico, a modern center of classical music, makes it exciting—and affordable—during the annual Festival Casals.

Because ticket prices are kept startlingly low (in order to encourage local students to attend), advance reservations are essential.

LeLoLai

The LeLoLai VIP initiative is a package of benefits that offers discounts at many attractions, and participating hotels, restaurants, and shops. The package costs just $10, but the savings can be more than $2,500 if you endeavor to use all the coupons. The package must be purchased after your arrival in Puerto Rico. Contact the Casita Tourist Office on your arrival, or call 723-3135 or 800-STAR (in the US) for more details.

Gambling

Although it's not Las Vegas, you will find casinos at all the major resort areas around the island. The majority are concentrated on the **Condado/Isla Verde** strip. The **Condado Plaza** on Ashord Avenue (Tel. 721-1000) and the **El San Juan Hotel** in Isla Verde (Tel. 791-0390) are two.

Most casinos are open daily—except for a few major holidays—from early afternoon until 4am. After dark, men are required to wear jackets (but not ties).

Nightlife

San Juan "never closes," they say, with pride. And they're absolutely right. Even at sunrise, you'll see bright-eyed people heading for an early breakfast after spending all night at a discotheque or nightclub that stays open until the last patron departs.

Puerto Ricans love entertainment, and they need no excuse to dress up, or generally let their hair down. This is the most switched-on island in the Caribbean for after-dark activities.

The large hotels in **Condado** and **Isla Verde** have supper clubs and lounges, discos and piano bars, and flamenco and *bomba y plena* shows for those who want a taste of traditional Puerto Rican culture. If you want to do some moving and shaking, there are discotheques and nightclubs galore.

Old San Juan, with its picturesque little musical spots hidden behind discreet wooden doors, doesn't hit high gear until after 10pm; Condado and Isla Verde get started somewhat earlier. On Friday and Saturday practically every place with entertainment imposes a drink purchase minimum. Some also levy a stiff, non-consumable cover charge. During the week, drink minimums are normally lowered or eliminated.

Calendar of Events

In addition to the many national celebrations, every town or village holds regular fiestas; each village also has a saint's day, honoring the patron saint of the local church. Festivals always involve a parade with costumes and masks, loud music, and good food. The following list gives the island's major festivals; check with the Casita Tourist office on the waterfront in San Juan for additional details. Information about local festivals is printed in *Qué Pasa*, available at tourist offices and hotels.

January. *Three King's Day (6th):* Parades and celebrations island-wide.

February. *Coffee Harvest Festivals:* In Maricao and Yauco (usually 13th–15th). *Ponce Carnival:* On the southern coast (5th–14th).

March. *Emancipation Day (22nd):* Celebrations to mark the freeing of the slaves.

March/April. *Semana Santa:* Outdoor processions and church services from Palm Sunday to Easter Sunday.

April. *Sugar Harvest Festival, San Germán:* (Dates vary.)

June. *San Juan Bautista Day:* Major festivities in San Juan and throughout the island honoring St. John the Baptist, Puerto Rico's patron saint. Week-long celebrations culminate on the day of the feast, the 24th.

July. *St. James Festival:* Almost two weeks of celebration on Vieques honoring that island's patron saint.

August. *International Billfish Tournament:* At the Club Nautico in San Juan.

September. *The Inter-American Arts Festival:* At the Centro de Bellas Artes in San Juan.

October. *Columbus Day (12th):* Commemorates the discovery of the New World.

November. *Bomba y Plena Festival, Ponce:* (Dates vary.) *Taíno Indian Festival, Jayuya:* Celebrates the culture of the Indians who lived on the island at the time of Columbus. *Festival of Puerto Rican Music, San Juan:* Traditional instruments and virtuoso performances.

December. *Festival of Masks, Hatillo:* Costumes and folk music combined with Christmas festivities.

For "big-name" entertainment, your best bet may be an all-inclusive dinner-show-dancing ticket. Resident singers and comedians perform and a dance troupe struts its stuff before you take to the dance floor yourself.

During the high (winter) season and on any weekend, you must reserve seats for a show or a popular restaurant. The biggest night-on-the-town is "social Friday" (which begins after work on Friday evening and doesn't end until breakfast time Saturday). If you're going anywhere in San Juan by car on Friday night, allow at least a half-hour extra to negotiate the traffic.

SPORTS

Beach Activities

Along the 365 miles (587 km) of Puerto Rican coastline you'll find all kinds of sandy beaches, some developed, many deserted. The resort beaches of **Dorado**, **Condado/Isla Verde**, and **Palmas del Mar** are enticing, offering wonderful soft sand and a comprehensive range of activities to choose from: you can arrange for kayaking, jet-skiing, and paragliding through the large hotels or the private companies situated on the beach.

In the northwest, around Rincón and Aguadilla, the waves build to giant heights; surfing and boogie-boarding is extremely popular. Don't expect to be able to surf in the south and east, however; because conditions there are not as favorable. Even in the northwest, the waves are best between January and March.

Golf

Puerto Rico has arguably the best golf in the Caribbean. With a number of championship courses and some two dozen 18-hole courses scattered across the countryside, it's quite possible to spend a week or two playing a different course every day. The greatest concentration of courses is at **Dorado**, west of

San Juan. The large Hyatt resorts here have invested heavily in recent years in upgrading and expanding courses that were already well regarded. They're all considered challenging.

All courses on Puerto Rico are open to the public or non-guests, with the exception of the El Conquistador at Fajardo, which is for hotel guests only. Here is a list of some of the better courses, working clockwise around the island from San Juan:

Bahia Beach Plantation (Río Grande; Tel. 256-5600). The course closest to San Juan.

Rio Mar Country Club (Río Grande; Tel. 888-8811).

Westin Rio Mar Beach Resort and Country Club (Río Grande; Tel. 888-6000).

Dorado Del Mar Golf Club (Dorado; Tel. 643-5997).

Hyatt Dorado Beach Golf Club (Dorado; Tel. 796-8961).

Hyatt Regency Cerromar Golf Club (Dorado; Tel. 796-9816).

El Conquistador Resort and Country Club (Fajardo; Tel. 863-1000). For hotel guests only.

Wyndham Palmas del Mar Golf Club (south of Humacao; Tel. 852-6000).

Aguirre Golf Club (east of Ponce; Tel. 853-4052).

Club Deportivo del Oeste (Cabo Rojo; Tel. 851-8880).

Punta Borinquén Golf Club (Aguadilla; Tel. 890-2987).

Diving and Snorkeling

Puerto Rico's waters offer genuine thrills for divers. The coral reefs on the continental shelf surrounding the island provide an ideal habitat for myriad exotic fish and marine mammals. And since Puerto Rico is on the migratory path of many species, depending on the time of year, you might also be able to view some non-native seasonal visitors while exploring the reefs and grottoes. Another attraction for members of the wet set is being able to investigate shipwrecks on the ocean bottom—well over

100 vessels are known to have sunk hereabouts since the days of the Spanish galleons. Remember to bring your dive certificate with you, as you will only be allowed to rent equipment and dive if you can prove your competence. Here are some of the most exciting dive sites around the islands:

Fajardo. This is the jumping-off point for dives around Vieques and Culebra and other smaller islands off Puerto Rico's east coast. Especially good for viewing turtles (breeding grounds are nearby) and coral formations.

Ponce. The sea wall that runs along the south coast between Caja de Muerto and Cayo Cardona offers exciting diving at relatively shallow depth, around 40 ft (12 m).

La Parguera. A great base for dives off the southwestern coast. Over 40 sites, including caves and sea walls.

The Best Beaches

Isla Verde. Just a minute from all the main resort hotels in San Juan, this beautiful white-sand beach is one of the most popular on the island.

Luquillo. This pretty balneario to the east of San Juan is one of the largest beaches on the island.

Boquerón. Palms and sea grapes fringe this arc of well-tended beach on the southwest coast. Beaches to the south, toward Cabo Rojo, are beautiful and natural—no facilities for humans, but plenty of fish and birds.

Crash Boat Beach, north of Aguadilla. At this popular spot in the northwest you'll be able to watch surfers strut their stuff and fishermen land their catches.

Sun Bay, Vieques. Fine public beaches with good facilities ring the bay on the southern coast of this offshore island.

Playa Flamenco, Culebra. Miles of white sand on the north shore of this tiny island off Puerto Rico's eastern coast. Only one of many fine beaches on Culebra.

Mona Island. This uninhabited island off the west coast offers pristine conditions for diving and snorkeling. A bonus: seal populations to enjoy.

If you'd like to learn how to dive while in Puerto Rico, you can contact one of a network of dive centers that offer training from beginner to professional levels. All centers are affiliated with one of the major certifying bodies; PADI (Professional Association of Diving Instructors) is the most common. You'll need five days to complete the requirements for the basic qualification, the Open Water certificate. Once you have this you'll be allowed to dive with an instructor to a depth of 60 ft (18 m), which opens up many dive sites around Puerto Rico to you.

Many centers also offer an introductory session, commonly known as the "Discover Scuba Program." This involves a morning or afternoon of theory and swimming pool work, which will give you the chance to try out the basic techniques. Many large hotels offer this "taster" to their guests. Here are a number of reputable dive companies around the island:

Dorado Marine Center (Dorado; Tel. 796-4654). Snorkeling, resort courses, and certification.

Caribbean School of Aquatics. (San Juan; Tel. 728-6606). Certification and dive trips, sailing, and exploring.

Mundo Submarino (Isla Verde; Tel. 791-5764). Daily diving tours and PADI training.

The best places for snorkeling are in the waters off of **Vieques**, **Culebra**, and **Mona Island**. Here the shallow waters have not been spoiled by too much human activity. Some of the nearer offshore cays also offer good opportunities: **Coffin Island** off the southern coast near Guánica and **Cat Island** off of La Parguera still have clear waters; both

One of the best beaches on the island, Isla Verde offers white sand, blue seas, and the chance to rise above it all.

are accessible via a short boat trip. The mangrove forests around the town of La Parguera also provide an interesting environment to explore; the tidal shallows there are a breeding ground for many species of fish.

Fishing

Sport fishing is very big in Puerto Rico, with several major tournaments being launched throughout the year from ports around the island. But if you're not ready to compete, boats for recreational fishing can be rented by the day or half day. If your base is San Juan, you'll only have to travel some 15 minutes out of **San Juan Harbor** to find a good catch. From **Fajardo** on the east coast there's excellent fishing in the waters around Culebra and Vieques (approximately 45 minutes from the port) and the US Virgin Islands. **La Parguera** is also a prime spot for big game fishing. From **Ponce** there's good fishing beyond the reef walls about an hour offshore. The peak season for billfish is May–October; for dolphin, tuna, and wahoo, November–April.

Sailing

The **Puerto del Rey Marina** near Fajardo has one of the largest charter-boat bases in the Caribbean—here you can arrange for a bare-boat charter, or a day-sail or power-boat rental. (They also service the San Juan area.) The **Caribbean School of Aquatics** in San Juan (Tel. 728-6606) has a 50-ft (15-m) catamaran for day sails. In **La Parguera** you can rent small power boats to explore the mangrove swamps, including Lovers Hole and the phosphorescent bay.

Hiking

Puerto Rico's natural and unspoiled interior offers lots of opportunity to get away from the city and commune with nature. With such a wealth of different environments to enjoy, it's well

Whether you want to win a medal or bring home dinner, there are spots to try your luck all along the island's coast.

worth making the effort to leave your hotel. **El Yunque** (the Caribbean National Forest), southeast of San Juan, is criss-crossed by numerous trails. The hike from the visitors center to La Mina Falls and back takes about an hour, but there are longer trails if you want to spend a whole day out. Stop by the El Portal Tropical Forest Center before setting out; guides are available, but you must request one in advance (Tel. 888-1880).

There are several other parks and forests throughout the island that have marked trails and facilities such as picnic tables:

Carite (Guavate) Forest. Between San Juan and Ponce, off Route 52. A 6000-acre (2,430-hectare) dwarf forest with trees no higher than 12 ft (3½ m); several high peaks and a lake.

Toro Negro Forest. North of Ponce. The highest point in Puerto Rico—Cerro de Punta, 4,390 ft (1,340 m)—lies within this reserve. The mountain can be scaled via a path off of Route 143; the ascent takes only about 40 minutes but on a clear day

Even the hardest-to-please travelers will find plenty of diversion an this kid-friendly island.

allows views all across the island. You are much more likely to get good weather here than on El Yunque (which acts as a magnet for moist winds traveling east across the Atlantic).

Guánica Forest. West of Ponce, off Route 2. This extremely arid and rocky area of land supports a large "dry tropical forest." Acres of cacti and ground-hugging plants support populations of over half of the bird species found in Puerto Rico.

Maricao. East of Mayagüez. This reserve has over 30 species of trees that grow only here.

CHILDREN

Young visitors to Puerto Rico can play for hours on the sandy beaches, jumping waves in the shallows or building sand castles. Condado/Isla Verde or Dorado have clean, safe beaches with good facilities and most of the *balnearios* have a children's play area with swings and see-saws, if they tire of the sea and sand. Older children can fill the whole day with snorkeling and learning about the numerous fish and marine creatures that teem in the shallow waters near the beaches.

Most large resort hotels offer activities for children; some may even have a children's club at which young visitors can make new friends and spend time in group activities like face-painting or organized water sports. Check with the hotel before making a reservation.

Always remember to cover young skin with a strong sunblock and to limit children's exposure time for the first few days. Also make sure that they are well supervised whenever they are near the water.

Here are some attractions and activities that score high points with younger visitors:

El Morro and San Cristóbal. Children enjoy walking the walls and parapets of these forts, imagining what it would have been like to be Spanish conquistadors.

Museo del Niño (Plazuela de las Monjas, opposite San Juan Cathedral; Tel. 722-3791). An engaging hands-on museum designed just for children. Open Tue–Thur 9am–3:30pm, Fri 9am–5pm, Sat and Sun 12:30–5pm.

Kite flying. Great fun for children of all ages.

Feeding the pigeons at Palomas Park. The birds in this Old San Juan park are almost tame and are sure to feed from the hand.

Festivals and street parades. Children thoroughly enjoy the spectacle, music, and dancing that is part of any Puerto Rican celebration. Check with the tourist office for details during your visit.

EATING OUT

Puerto Rico's remarkable array of food ranges all the way from exotic Caribbean through continental European to everyday American, not to mention Chinese, Argentine, and Thai. You will be able to find all the standard international dishes in hotel restaurants and in many city eateries. But it is the selection of native island dishes that is both surprising and pleasing because it stands on its own merits as a style of cuisine. Puerto Rican *criollo* cooking is a fascinating blend of Amerindian ingredients and techniques combined with Spanish and European influences.

Where to Eat

For variety, quality, and, probably, economy as well, you should head out from your hotel for at least part of your stay to

Asopao, tostones, and rice—and this is just the first course in Puerto Rican criollo cuisine.

enjoy some local dishes. San Juan has sit-at-the-counter "lun-cheonettes" open far into the night. Some of the best local food is served in rather bland and old-fashioned surroundings; the taste and quality of the food are the only things that matter. Puerto Ricans sit for hours chatting under the strip lights, oblivious to the plastic counters and linoleum. Yet there are also smart, chic eateries serving the most fashionable dishes. Closing day for most restaurants is either Sunday or Monday.

Neither Americans nor Europeans will find eating here inexpensive—except perhaps at the well-known US fast food chains. One reason for this is that surprisingly little is grown on Puerto Rico, so many things have to be imported. Native cooking, of course, takes full advantage of what's available locally.

What to Eat

Street Food

Puerto Ricans live life on the street and on the go, and they've devised a number of favorite foods that can be prepared and eaten at small kiosks on city sidewalks, at beaches, and at roadside cafés. You'll see people eating as they go about their business, or sitting in city squares enjoying a quick lunch. The best-loved street snacks are *bacalaítos fritos* (deep-fried codfish fritters), *pastelillos* or *empanadillas* (crescent shaped deep-fried meat and cheese turnovers), *plátanos* (plantains, similar to bananas), *alcapurrias* or *mofongos* (croquettes stuffed with beef or pork), *surrullitos de maíz* (deep-fried cornmeal sticks), and *pastelones* (meat pies).

Small pieces of meat or chicken fried and served on a skewer with *plátanos tostones* (fried plantains) are called "*pinchos*" (*de carne* or *de pollo*). These are the single-serving fast-food version of a full barbecued animal, which is a favorite with the Puertorriqueños.

Puerto Rico's Specialties

Island recipes, many of them Taíno Indian dishes that have been refined over the centuries, are proof that beans, rice, root vegetables, and fruit need not be dull. Normally food here is only mildly spicy but intriguing, thanks to two distinctly criollo blends of seasoning: *sofrito* and *adobo*. Both begin with a foundation of oil, garlic, and oregano. Sofrito also has salt pork, cured ham, onion, chili peppers, and green pepper, while adobo adds crushed black pepper and either vinegar or fresh lime juice.

Fish and seafood. The Puertorriqueños makes the most of the bounty of the surrounding seas. The catch of the day will always be fresh and delicious. Island favorites include *chillo* (red snapper), *macarela* (mackerel), *merluza* (hake), *cabrilla* (grouper), *mero* (sea bass), *chapín* (trunkfish), and *pulpo* (octopus). Other popular menu items include imported *atún* (tuna), *bacalao* (codfish), and *lenguado* (sole). Local *jueyes* (land crabs) are considered a delicacy.

Snapper and some other local fish may be proudly presented *de modo isleño*, sautéed in an elaborate sauce including olives, onions, tomato, capers, vinegar, garlic, and pimentos. A simpler option is to have the fillet sautéed with garlic and served with fresh lemon juice.

You'll find tasty, locally harvested *camarones* (shrimp) served as cold appetizers or snacks, or in hot entrées. *Langosta* (Caribbean spiny lobster), plentiful in the surrounding waters, isn't considered as tasty as the cold-water variety, which can be found in finer restaurants, but at quite a premium.

Barbecue. One of the most popular methods of cooking is the barbecue, developed from the traditional Indian technique called *barbacoa*. On any weekend you'll find families setting up their portable fires at the beach; and most roadside restaurants and snack bars have spits. At holiday time it's traditional for these establishments to roast a whole pig (*lechón achado*) and numerous whole chickens. *Chicharrones* are small pieces of pork with crunchy skin still attached, considered to be tastier than the flesh itself.

The banana family. Unlike their close cousin the *guineo* (the sweet banana), ubiquitous *plátanos* (plantains), a top island favorite, should not be eaten raw. Sliced green plantains may be deep-fried and eaten as an hors d'oeuvre (*tostones*); these are the standard accompaniment to street food. Both *amarillos* (yellow plantains)

Fresh, exotic fruit and vegetables can be had from any number of roadside vendors.

and delicious *guineos verdes* (green bananas) are often boiled. You may even be introduced to *guineo verde en escabeche* (pickled green banana) or baked, stuffed, or candied plantains. The leaves of the plantain or banana tree are used to wrap *pasteles,* the island's beloved boiled packets of seasoned pork, cured ham, *garbanzos* (chickpeas), chopped olives, and spices.

Fruit. Puerto Rico produces many varieties of fruit. Its pineapples are said to be the sweetest in the world, but you'll also be tempted by fresh coconuts, papayas, mangos, limes, tamarinds, breadfruit, and mammee apples, all available from roadside stalls. In restaurants you'll be able to enjoy them in fresh fruit salads, which are particularly refreshing for breakfast or for dessert. You'll also find watermelon and most familiar citrus fruits.

A Full Meal

Appetizers. Soups are a popular way to start a meal in Puerto Rico. The classic, which you'll find on many menus across the island, is *sopa de habichuelas negras* or *de frijoles negros* (black bean); in some places it can have a thick, almost stew-like consistency, but it should always contain wine and garlic and be garnished with chopped onions. You can also find *sopa de pollo con arroz* (chicken soup with rice), or *sopa de pescado* (fish soup), made with whatever variety of fish has been caught locally on the day. An amazing number of ingredients, notably local vegetables, plantains, and meats, go into *sancocho,* known in English as Caribbean soup. If you see it on a menu, it's definitely worth trying.

Another very popular soup is *asopao*. In most places it's so rich and hearty you could make a meal out of it. Flavored with garlic and paprika, it is full of meat, rice, seasonal vegetables, and whatever else the cook might be inspired to add. There are many variations on the asopao theme—each chef seems to have his or her own recipe.

Two other authentically native dishes to try as a first course (if you're feeling adventurous) are *sierra en escabeche* (pickled kingfish), served cold, and *morcillas* (blood sausages).

Main courses. Rice figures prominently in many other island favorites, such as the Spanish standbys *paella* and *arroz con pollo* (chicken with rice). Perhaps the most innovative meat dish you'll find is *piononos*—ripe plantains, chopped meat, eggs, and tomato paste cooked in *salsa criolla* (creole sauce). *Carne mechada*, translated on San Juan menus as "eye round beef," resembles a bland stuffed pot roast. Less routine is *cabro* (kid or young goat), probably fricasseed. Meats are often served breaded (*empanada*).

Hearty, filling stews are also to be found on many menus: *caldo gallego* (Galician broth) is a Spanish import made of salt pork, ham, *chorizo* (spicy sausage), and white beans and turnips, while *sopa de garbazonas con patas de cerdo* is a local invention made of chickpeas and pig's feet. Traditional recipes like these make the most of all parts of the animal, so it's not unheard of to find brains, feet, tongue, or other organs in the list of ingredients.

For those looking for a relatively simple, light entrée, a Puerto Rican chef can always turn out an excellent *tortilla española* (Spanish omelet), which might include chopped *chorizo* or shrimp.

Side dishes. You'll find an exotic array of local vegetables with names such as *chayote, yuca, yautía,* and *ñame,* all categorized as *verduras* (greens) and often served in stews. Humble *arroz con frijoles* (rice and beans), perhaps the most popular side dish, can be a real treat when prepared by native chefs here. *Amarillos en dulce* (yellow plantains fried in butter, cinnamon, sugar, and red wine) make an unexpectedly tasty accompaniment to a meal.

Desserts. The two Puerto Rican dessert staples, *flan* (custard) and the much ballyhooed coconut version, *tembleque,* don't usually tempt a visitor more than once. More intriguing choices include *dulce de lechosa con queso blanco* (papaya cubes cooked in sugar and cinnamon with white cheese) or *arroz con dulce* or *con coco* (boiled rice in coconut cream, with sugar and cinnamon). You can find ice-cream, either the major US names or local producers, in a variety of flavors.

Coffee is the standard after-dinner beverage. While the amount of the highest quality crop is small, the lesser blends are still very good, being smoother than the average Colombian blend. Islanders order *pocillo negro* (black demitasse) after meals rather than the *café con leche* (a large cup with half coffee, half milk) popular at other times of day. Most places offer both the strong local coffee and the weaker American brew.

Spirits

Puerto Rico styles itself as the "**rum capital of the world**," and, as you'd expect, island hotels pride themselves on using the local product in as many interesting ways as possible. To test the local wisdom that rum goes with anything, there are literally dozens of drinks you can

In Puerto Rico, the local bar almost rivals the town square as a social center.

try. Every barman will have his own special concoction and you are bound to be greeted by a member of staff offering a complimentary rum punch soon after you check in. Despite all this variety and innovation, however, the **piña colada** (see page 35) remains Puerto Rico's gift to the world; invented here in the 1950s, this sublime blend of rum, coconut, and pineapple juice is now enjoyed all over the globe.

Most of the rum cocktails are strong, so remember to pace yourself. The light, blending rums, though the most popular, are not the only ones produced on the island. All the major producers—**Don Q** and **Bacardi** are the best known—also produce sipping rums, aged in oak for up to 12 years. These are enjoyed just as a fine cognac or scotch would be, drunk neat or over ice. Despite the fact that rum is produced in huge quantities here, it's not much cheaper than the full range of other spirits that are also readily available.

You'll find a reasonable range of Californian and Chilean wines on offer in bars and restaurants, though the finest is often very expensive. Most beer drinkers find the local brands quite acceptable; **Medalla** is the major brand. The best selling American and some European beers are available but always cost more than the domestic brands.

To Help You Order...

Do you have a set menu?   ¿**Tiene un menú del día?**
I'd like a/an/some…   **Quisiera…**

beans	**frijoles**	menu	**menú**
beer	**una cerveza**	milk	**leche**
bread	**pan**	mineral water	**agua mineral**
cheese	**queso**	potatoes	**papas**
chicken	**pollo**	rice	**arroz**
coffee	**un café**	salad	**una ensalada**
dessert	**un postre**	sandwich	**un sandwich**
eggs	**huevos**	shellfish	**mariscos**
fish	**pescado**	soup	**una sopa**
fruit	**fruta**	sugar	**azúcar**
glass	**un vaso**	tea	**un té**
ice-cream	**un mantecado**	water (iced)	**agua (fría)**
meat	**carne**	wine	**vino**

...and Read the Menu

aceitunas	olives	guineo	banana
aguacate	avocado	jueyes	land crabs
atún	tuna	langosta	spiny lobster
almejas	clams	langostino	prawn
anchoas	anchovies	lenguado	sole
asado	roast	limón	lemon
bacalao	codfish	mamey	mammee apple
bacalaítos	codfish	manzana	apple
fritos	fritters	melocotón	peach
batata	white sweet	mejillones	mussels
dulce	potato	mero	sea bass
biftec	beef steak	morcillas	blood sausages
bizcocho	cake	ñame	yam
cabrito	young goat	naranja	orange
calabaza	squash	ostras	oysters
calamares	squid	piña	pineapple
camarones	shrimp	plátanos	plantains
cangrejo	crab	platános	yellow
cerdo	pork	amarillos	plantains
chillo	red snapper	pulpo	octopus
cordero	lamb	salchichón	salami
chorizo	pork sausage	salsa	sauce
chuletas	chops	sancocho	Caribbean
escabeche	pickled		stew
filete	fillet	surrullitos	cornmeal
frambuesas	raspberries		sticks
fresas	strawberries	tembleque	coconut
frito	fried		custard
garbanzos	chickpeas	ternera	veal
granadas	pomegranates	tortilla	omelet
guayaba	guava	tostones	fried plantains

INDEX

HANDY TRAVEL TIPS

An A–Z Summary of Practical Information

A

ACCOMMODATIONS (See CAMPING and YOUTH HOSTELS)

Puerto Rico has a full range of accommodations, from small city hotels to luxury beach resorts to historic buildings and plantation houses that have been converted into charming lodgings full of character. You'll encounter several different kinds of room-and-meal-plan packages: AI (All-Inclusive) means that all resort services and activities, sports facilities, meals, and drinks are included in the price. AP (American Plan) provides breakfast, lunch, and dinner along with lodging, whereas MAP (Modified American Plan) provides only breakfast and dinner. EP (European Plan) rates are for the room alone, without meals.

Many of the larger resorts and hotels are clustered in pockets around the island. By far the biggest are at **Isla Verde** and **Condado**, east of San Juan. These two areas, once separate, have now merged into one long strip of hotels, condos, and motels. Here you'll rub shoulders with millions of your fellow visitors, but you'll also find myriad restaurants and shops, as well as fantastic beaches, all on your doorstep. These resorts are within easy reach of the city of Old San Juan. Many large resorts offer sports facilities and activities such as golf courses and scuba diving lessons and guided dives. Some include access to all sports facilities in the price; others charge for each activity separately, above the room rate. Many resorts also offer wedding packages and honeymoon specials.

Two other resort areas are growing rapidly. **Dorado**, about 30 minutes west of San Juan by car, and **Palmas del Mar**, about an hour southeast of San Juan, both have good hotel facilities. It pays to rent a car for your stay in either of these areas, though, because, apart from the facilities and restaurants at the resorts, there are few options in either spot for dining and exploring under your own steam.

In other parts of the island, large hotels with a range of facilities are limited in number and the other option, **paradores** (small country inns), have no guaranteed standards of facilities, furnishings, or service. The Puerto Rico Tourism Company backs a number of paradores throughout the island. Unfortunately, there is no uniform standard in Puerto Rico, and many paradores do not live up to the images the promoters attempt to portray, being in some cases neither small nor rustic. This is a pity, since some are highly interesting places to stay, and while not up to 5-star standards, they bring you closer to the real Puerto Rico. A number are listed in Recommended Hotels on page 130. For a complete list, contact the Puerto Rico Tourism Company; for reservations, call 721-2884 or 800-443-0266.

It's important to make reservations to guarantee you get the kind of lodging you want, especially between November and April, when most of the most popular hotels operate at almost 100% occupancy. During the summer it should be possible to negotiate a discount on room rates since hotels operate at below capacity. All hotels add a room tax. This varies from 8–11% depending on the establishment.

AIRPORTS

Puerto Rico's main airport is the **Luis Muñoz Marín International Airport** (Tel. 791-4670), approximately 20 minutes east of downtown San Juan, just 10 minutes from Isla Verde. The taxis outside the arrivals terminal charge standard fares for trips to the resorts or into town (Isla Verde $8, Condado $12, Old San Juan $16). All major car rental companies operate shuttles from outside the arrivals area to their compounds on the airport's perimeter.

There are smaller airports in **San Juan** (Isla Grande, just off San Juan harbor; Tel. 729-8711), **Ponce** (Aeropeuerto Mercedita; Tel. 842-6292), **Mayagüez** (Aeropuerto Eugenio Maria de Hostos; Tel. 833-0148), **Aguadilla** (Rafael Hernández Airport; Tel. 891-2286), **Vieques** (Aeropuerto Rivera Rodriguez; Tel. 741-0515), and **Culebra** (Aeropuerto Benjiamin Rivera Noriega; Tel. 742-0022). There are regular internal flights to each of these airports on American Eagle and local small carriers. Flights to Culebra and Vieques leave from Isla Grande Airport on San Juan Bay.

B

BUDGETING For YOUR TRIP

The resorts of Puerto Rico can be expensive. Among other things, many foodstuffs must be imported, which results in a price premium in many of the resorts and fine hotels. The cost of food outside of the hotels, however, is little different from that on mainland US; in the countryside it's possible to eat very inexpensively at local restaurants.

The following list will give you an idea of the average prices for services and activities:

Accommodations. A room in a resort or luxury hotel, $250 per night. Room in a moderately priced hotel, $140. Room in an inexpensive hotel, $80. Paradores out in the island can be a real bargain; some charge as little as $50 a night. All hotels add a lodging tax. This varies between 8–11%.

Boat rental. Fishing charter $600 per day; small dinghy $15 per hour.

Car rental. Daily rates start at around $40 per day, rising to around $90 for compact cars in high season.

Dinner. The cost of a three-course dinner, without drinks, ranges between $50 per person in a fine restaurant to $35 per person in a mid-range establishment to $20 per person in an inexpensive eatery.

Diving. Two-tank dives from around $70; certification courses from $450.

Ferries. The ride from Fajardo to Vieques, $2 one-way.

Golf. Greens fee at Palmas del Mar ranges from $90 to $130 per person, depending on the season.

Taxis. From Muñoz Marín Airport to the resorts at Isla Verde, $8; to Condado, $12; to Old San Juan, $16.

C

CAMPING

There are options for camping all across the island, many in the park areas. You can choose from basic cabins and camping sites where you can pitch your own tent. Most of the cabins can áccommodate about six people. You can reserve one through the Recreational Development Company in Puerto Rico (Tel. 721-2800).

CAR RENTAL

Puerto Rico is an island of many contrasts, and unless you only intend to take a short break from a stay in San Juan or one of the resorts (where taxi service is good), you'll need a car to really see all of island's glories, especially the mountains of the interior. There are a number of points to take into consideration, however, before you set off into the hills (see DRIVING); drivers of a sensitive disposition should probably not take to the roads at all.

There is a wide choice when it comes to car-rental companies in Puerto Rico, but many of the local companies rent older vehicles and do not offer a network of support should you run into mechanical trouble on the road. Always beware of cheap deals. It is far wiser to opt for a well-known company that can offer full back-up in case of problems.

Most of the major rental companies have offices at Muñoz Marín Airport and at various locations in San Juan, Ponce, and Mayagüez. If you intend to arrive in peak season, it's best to reserve a vehicle in advance. Prices start at around $40 per day for a compact car, rising to around $90 at peak season.

Drivers must be over 21 and carry a valid driver's license; some smaller companies stipulate a minimum age of 25. All rental agreements offer damage waiver and personal insurance as extras. Extra insurance is advisable. Collision Damage Waiver (CDW) will cover you against any damage to your rental car. If your credit card does not include insurance cover for rental cars (your domestic vehicle policy may also cover rental in Puerto Rico), it's important to indemnify yourself against damage. The cost of CDW is around $15 per day.

Here are some of the major companies with offices in Puerto Rico:

Avis	Tel. 721-4499 or 800-874-3556
Budget	Tel. 791-3685 or 800-527-0700
Hertz	Tel. 791-0840 or 800-645-3030
Thrifty	Tel. 253-2525 or 800-367-2277

I'd like to rent a car for one day/one week.	**Quisiera alquilar un auto por un día/por una semana.**
Please include full insurance.	**Haga el favor de incluir el seguro completo.**
Driver's license	**Licencia de conducir**
Car registration papers	**Papeles del registro del auto**

CLIMATE

Puerto Rico has a marine tropical climate, which offers fine warm-to-hot weather all year round. Temperatures rarely rise above the upper 80s Fahrenheit (mid-20s Celsius) and they rarely dip below the low 70s. Even in the heat of summer (May–Oct), trade winds cool the beaches and hillsides, though the towns can become hot and stifling. The mountains are always a few degrees cooler than the coastal plains.

The rainy season, though it hardly merits the name, is officially in the summer, the low season for tourism in Puerto Rico. Rainfall averages approximately 69 inches (177 cm) per year, coming in short but intense tropical storms. Far more rain falls in the higher verdant east than in the dryer west.

The official hurricane season is from 1 June to 30 November. Forecasters can now locate storms thousands of miles away, which gives locals and visitors ample time to leave the islands if danger threatens. Call 253-0840 for a weather forecast.

The following chart gives the average monthly temperatures and rainfall for the island:

	J	F	M	A	M	J	J	A	S	O	N	D
Temperature °C	25	24	24	24	25	26	26	26	26	26	26	25
Temperature °F	78	77	77	77	78	80	80	80	80	80	80	78
Rainfall inches	4	3	2	4	7	6	6	6	6	6	6	6

CLOTHING

You should have no trouble packing a wardrobe for your trip to the Puerto Rico. Beach attire is a must, as are comfortable wraps or cover-ups for around the hotel. Don't wear anything too skimpy if you head into town; most local people dress modestly. Light cottons or silks make the best fabrics, being breathable and cool. Don't forget a hat, sunglasses, and sunscreen, because the sun is very powerful here.

If you intend to hike or walk in the countryside, it would be wise to take a long sleeved shirt to guard against the sun or insect bites and a sweater or fleece jacket, because when clouds descend it can turn chilly. It's best to have stout shoes in the uncertain terrain—the mountain trails can be muddy and in karst country the surface can be very uneven.

One thing Puerto Rican men and women have in common is that they enjoy dressing up, be it for a wedding, a party, or simply a night on the town. If you intend to visit a fine restaurant, the theater, or a casino, it would be wise to pack a couple of smart outfits. Women can go to town if they wish, as sequins and stilettos are not unknown here.

COMPLAINTS

Complaints should always be taken up first with the establishment or individual concerned. If this is unsuccessful, then take your complaint to the local Puerto Rican Tourism Company office; they should be able to advise you further.

The Tourist Police can be contacted at Tel. 772-0738. For tourist complaints; Tel. 721-2400.

CRIME and SAFETY

Crime has certainly been a problem in the main tourist areas in recent years. Puerto Rico is a major conduit for drugs traveling to the US from South America, and this, along with local gang rivalries, has caused problems for police and security officials. Petty crime, muggings, and car theft increased in the last few years in the Isla Verde and Condado area. The authorities have made great strides, however, in preventing crime and increasing visitor confidence. Regular police forces make numerous patrols, and a special Tourist Police force monitors the streets and beaches in the resort areas. Their presence is very reassuring, but it's still wise to follow common sense and exercise sensible precautions when traveling around the resorts and the city.

Do not answer your hotel door without ascertaining who the visitor is. Always lock hotel doors, whether you're in or out. Do not tell casual acquaintances your room number, and do not leave keys lying around with your room number in view.

Never carry large amounts of cash or valuables and always use the hotel or cruise ship safe. Walk only along well-lit streets at night, in a group if possible. Use official taxis only—do not accept lifts from someone who stops to offer you a ride.

Put all valuables out of sight when leaving your vehicle, or even better, take them with you. Always park in a busy lot or street. Do not leave valuables on the beach when you go for a swim, and do not walk along the beaches at night.

CUSTOMS and ENTRY REGULATIONS

Travelers to Puerto Rico from the US require only a valid, up-to-date form of identification; they do not need to prove citizenship. Canadian citizens need some form of photo ID along with proof of citizenship such as a voter registration card or birth certificate.

Travelers from other countries are required to clear US immigration. This may take place on the US mainland—if that's your port of entry and you're making a connection to San Juan. All passengers must carry a valid passport. A visa or green card may be required for travelers whose governments have made arrangements to operate under the visa-waiver scheme. Visitors are granted entry for 90 days. Those carrying a green visa-waiver form—which must stay in the passport at all times—should surrender it at the end of their stay.

Visas are required by all except residents of the EU (not including Greece and Portugal) and New Zealand.

South African nationals need a visa; they should contact the United States Embassy (P.O. Box 9536, 877 Pretorious Street, Pretoria, South Africa; Tel. 12/342-1048; fax 12/342-2299).

Travelers from the continental US do not need to pass through customs when entering Puerto Rico and can therefore take any items with them. For foreign visitors, items for personal use can be brought in duty-free; this includes 40 oz of liquor. Customs ask that you declare cash valued at more than $10,000. The head of each family group must also complete a customs declaration form.

 D

DRIVING

Driving in Puerto Rico is an adventure, and for some a nightmare. Timid drivers should consider finding alternative means of transportation. Puerto Rican drivers are notorious for driving with their own rules. Driving requires concentration, because vehicles will pull out in your path, pull or turn off without indication, or simply stop on the highway with little warning. Pedestrians also appear to act recklessly, often stepping out in front of you with only a cursory glance in your direction. Both drivers and pedestrians operate on subtle signals and messages that visitors may not understand.

In the countryside, chickens and dogs share the roadway. Roads twist and turn so that it's not always possible to see what waits around the bend. This does not deter local drivers, however, who often drive far faster than either the speed limit or common sense seem to dictate.

Road signs are not well placed. You may not see any indication of the road numbers or names until after you've made the turn. In cities many street names have been obliterated by stickers or painted over. On the new toll roads many exits are not signposted. It really is necessary to have a good map and to pay careful attention at all times when navigating.

Puerto Rico

If you need help there is no national service to come to your aid. Ask your rental agency for a number to call in case of breakdown, but don't expect someone to come out and rescue you within minutes, especially if you have broken down in the countryside.

Many rules of driving are the same as those in the US, though most signs are in Spanish. Distances on signs are expressed in kilometers, though speed limits are posted in miles per hour. The speed limit on the *autopistas* (highways) is 70 mph (112 km/h); in urban areas it's between 30 and 40 mph (48–64 km/h). Local drivers tend to ignore these limits.

Parking is difficult in cities. Do not park anywhere with a yellow curb. On many side streets parking is for residents only at certain times of day, so check for signs. The main car park in old San Juan is at Recinto Sur. Most large hotels have parking though many charge a daily fee for its use; they also offer valet parking at extra cost.

Fuel costs around 10%–15% more than on the US mainland (still a good deal less expensive than prices in Europe).

Fluid measures

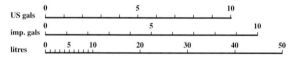

Distance

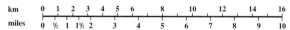

Here is a list of typical road signs you might encounter:

A la derecha con luz roja	Right turn on red light
Autopista	Thruway (divided highway)
Calle sin salida	Dead-end street (cul de sac)
Carril exclusivo guaguas	Bus lane only
Ceda el paso	Yield the right of way

Confluencia	Merging traffic
Cruce de peatones	Pedestrian crossing
Desvío	Detour
Escuela	School
Lomo	Bump, ridge
No entre	Do not enter
No estacione	No parking
No vire	No turn
Parada de guaguas	Bus stop
Pare	Stop
Peaje	Toll station
Peligro	Danger
Resbala mojado	Slippery when wet
Salida	Exit
Velocidad maxima	Speed limit
Zona escolar	School zone

Here are some useful phrases for when you are out on the road:

Are we on the right road for…	**¿Es ésta la carretera hacia…?**
Full tank, please.	**Llénelo, por favor.**
Check the oil/ tires/battery, please.	**Por favor, revise el aceite/ las gomas/la batería.**
There's been an accident.	**Hubo un accidente.**
I've had a breakdown.	**Mi auto se ha rotó.**

ELECTRICITY

The current in Puerto Rico is 110-volt, 60 cycles (the same as in North America). Travelers from the US and Canada will not need adapters for their appliances. Other visitors will need standard US adapters.

EMBASSIES and CONSULATES

A number of national consulates operate in Puerto Rico. Travelers from countries not represented on the island should contact the appropriate offices on the American mainland (most embassies and consulates are in Washington, DC).

Canada	Consul, Scotia Bank Plaza, Cereipo Street 107, Alturas de Santa Maria, Guaynabo, PR 00969; Tel. 790-2210; fax 790-2205.
UK	Consul, American Airlines Building, 11th Floor Suite 1100, López Ladrón Street 1509, Santurce PR 00911; Tel. 721-5193; fax 723-6965.

EMERGENCIES

Dial 911 for emergency calls.

G

GAY and LESBIAN TRAVELERS

Puerto Rico is one of the most gay-friendly destinations in the Caribbean, and the scene in the capital is particularly diverse and lively. **Old San Juan** is home to a number of night-spots, restaurants, and boutique hotels favored by gay travelers; **Casa del Caribe** (Tel. 722-7139) is one of the favorite gathering spots here. The center of gay life in Condado is the **Atlantic Beach Hotel** (Tel. 721-6900), which has a number of restaurants and bars on site. Another popular locus is the **Ocean Park Beach** area, between Old San Juan and Condado, which now has several gay guest houses as well as the city's most popular gay and lesbian beach (at the end of Calle Santa Ana). Finally, the **Santurce** district, east of Miramar and south of Condado, is home to two of the hottest dance clubs: **Music People** (316 Avenida de Diego; Tel. 724-2123) and **Eros** (1257 Avenida Ponce de León; Tel. 722-1131).

The monthly magazine *Puerto Rico Breeze*, available for free at clubs, bars, and hotels, is full of listings, news, and helpful advice for gay visitors.

GETTING TO PUERTO RICO

By air. Puerto Rico is the major gateway airport between North and South America and many other islands in the Caribbean. Almost all international flights arrive at **Luis Muñoz Marín International Airport**, which is about 30 minutes east of Old San Juan, on the outskirts of the modern city.

American Airlines (Tel. 800-474-4884 or 749-1747) has direct flights to San Juan from several major US cities, including Miami, New York, Chicago, Dallas, Philadelphia, and Washington. **American Eagle** (Tel. 800-474-4884 or 749-1747) offers a number of internal flights within Puerto Rico and to other Caribbean islands. Other airlines that operate from the US include **Delta** (Tel. 800-221-1212), which runs four flights a day from Atlanta, **USAir** (Tel. 800-428-4322), which provides direct service from Philadelphia and Baltimore, **United** (Tel. 800-241-6522 or 253-2276), which offers direct flights from Chicago in addition to connections from East Coast cities, and **TWA** (Tel. 800-892-4141 or 253-0440).

From Europe, **British Airways** (Tel. 800-247-9297 or 723-4327; in UK, 345-222111) and **Lufthansa** (Tel. 800-645-3880) both run one flight a week to San Juan. **Iberia** (Tel. 800-221-1212) offers two flights a week from Madrid. Most European travelers find it more convenient to make connections through Miami or New York.

Visitors from Australia and New Zealand should travel through the US to reach Puerto Rico. Both the east- and west-bound trips involve stopovers.

Vieques Air Link (Tel. 722-3736) and **Air Nena** (Tel. 741-6362) offer flights from Isla Grande to Vieques. **Flamenco Airways** (Tel. 725-7707) runs flights from Isla Grande to Culebra.

By sea. San Juan is one of the busiest cruise ports in the world, with several large ships arriving and departing each week (it's been reported that over 50% of all cruises stop or depart from this port). Most ships arrive from Miami, but some cruises also depart from San Juan (with air links from the US or Europe). Among the cruise operators with the largest number of tour options are **Celebrity Cruises** (Tel. 800-437-3111 or 305/262-8322; UK 0500-332-232);

Puerto Rico

Norwegian Cruise Line (Tel. 800-327-7030; UK 0800-181-560;
Royal Caribbean Cruise Line (Tel. 800-327-6700; UK 0500-212-
213); and **Carnival Cruise Lines** (Tel. 800-439-6744).

GUIDES and TOURS

Colonial Adventures (210 Calle Ricento Sur, San Juan; Tel. 774-
9919; website <www.caribead.com/colonial.html>) offers guided
walking tours of Old San Juan. **Castillo Tours** (2413 Calle Laurel,
Punta las Marias, Santurce, San Juan; Tel. 791-6195) runs excursions
to El Yunque, Ponce, the Camuy Caves, and other attractions on the
island, as well as sailing trips to Vieques. Half-day tours start at $30
per person. For walking and adventure tours, contact **Encantos
Ecotours** (Tel. 272-0005).

H

HEALTH and MEDICAL CARE

Puerto Rico is generally a healthy and safe place to vacation, provided
you take a few sensible precautions. First of all, go easy on the alcohol,
especially in the sunshine, as this could lead to dehydration. Take time
in building a tan to avoid sunburn and sunstroke; the sea breezes that
blow across the island can lull you into a sense of false security. If hiking (and perhaps even walking around the old town) take plenty of liq-
uid to avoid dehydration. There are also some minor nuisances that
should be avoided. Mosquitoes can be a problem, especially toward
sundown, so cover up or apply insect repellent. Sand flies, called "no
see 'ums" because they are so small, can bite, so carry repellent with
you at all times just in case you run into some. Be careful not to step on
spiny sea urchins while you're snorkeling or diving; the spines will
embed themselves into your flesh and they can become infected. Do not
touch any creatures or coral under the water; some are toxic.

If you need any medical treatment, you will need to be able to show
that you can afford to pay for the treatment, either from your own funds
or through insurance. Always make sure that you have adequate insurance to cover any medical emergency. Each of the major towns on the

island has a clinic or medical center that can offer 24 hour emergency care or care for non-critical conditions. All major hotels have a doctor on call 24 hours a day; you will be asked to pay a consultation fee.

In the event of an emergency, dial **911** for help, or, in San Juan, one of the following numbers: **Police**; Tel. 434-2020. **Ambulance**; Tel. 434-2550. **Fire department**, Tel. 434-2330.

HITCHHIKING

Hitchhiking is not advised. In recent years, there have been attacks on tourists, particularly in metropolitan San Juan.

 L

LANGUAGE

Spanish is the first language in Puerto Rico. Because of the growing influence of US cable TV, however, you're likely to hear a good deal of "Spanglish"—a blend of Spanish and English vocabulary and grammar—in everyday conversational speech. Most Puerto Ricans working in tourist-related positions speak excellent English and you will have no difficulty even if you don't speak Spanish.

People in the major towns speak some English (every schoolchild has 50 minutes of English every day), but once in the interior don't expect everyone to understand English. (Also see the language tips on the front cover flap).

Days of the week

Sunday	**domingo**	Thursday	**jueves**
Monday	**lunes**	Friday	**viernes**
Tuesday	**martes**	Saturday	**sábado**
Wednesday	**miércoles**		

Months

January	**enero**	March	**marzo**
February	**febrero**	April	**abril**
May	**mayo**	September	**septiembre**

Puerto Rico

June	**junio**	October	**octubre**
July	**julio**	November	**noviembre**
August	**agosto**	December	**diciembre**

Numbers

0	**cero**	19	**diecinueve**
1	**uno**	20	**veinte**
2	**dos**	21	**veintiuno**
3	**tres**	22	**veintidós**
4	**cuatro**	30	**treinta**
5	**cinco**	31	**trienta y uno**
6	**seis**	40	**cuarenta**
7	**siete**	50	**cincuenta**
8	**ocho**	60	**sesenta**
9	**nueve**	70	**setenta**
10	**diez**	80	**ochenta**
11	**once**	90	**noventa**
12	**doce**	100	**cien**
13	**trece**	101	**ciento uno**
14	**catorce**	200	**doscientos**
15	**quince**	1,000	**mil**
16	**dieciséis**	2,000	**dos mil**
17	**diecisiete**	1,000,000	**el millón**
18	**dieceocho**	2,000,000	**dos millones**

LAUNDRY and DRY CLEANING

Each major town has laundry and dry cleaning services, which are reliable and less expensive than hotel laundry service. Dry cleaners also offer express service.

M

MAPS

The Puerto Rico Tourism Company produces a magazine called *Qué Pasa,* which includes a useful map of Old San Juan with enough detail to allow you to design your own walking tour. It also includes a map of the whole island, though it's not detailed enough to use for driving.

MEDIA

Puerto Rico has a number of Spanish-language channels. The major ones are WKAQ, WAPA, WIPR, and WSTE. The main American cable channels are also widely available and most hotels have cable, which includes all the major channels. The primary daily Spanish newspaper is *El Nuevo Día*. The *San Juan Star* is published in English. The major American dailies are available from the larger news agents and in many hotels. European newspapers, when available, are usually a day old.

MONEY

Puerto Rico uses the US dollar as its currency (though you may hear older people still referring to their money as pesos). There are banks in all the major towns, though there are many more places to exchange money in the capital than in the countryside. It's advisable to change cash into dollars before arriving in Puerto Rico. There are currency exchange facilities at Muñoz Marín Airport. You'll find international **ATMs** in major towns throughout the island. Banco Popular has a good network, though other banks also provide this service. Most machines accept internationally recognized credit cards and cash cards for withdrawals. Look for the Cirrus and Plus signs on the ATM kiosks.

   Travelers' checks are still widely accepted, though some banks will charge a premium to cash them and they are more difficult to cash outside the capital. Always carry travelers' checks in US dollars rather than in other currencies. Major **credit cards** are accepted in most establishments (shops and restaurants), though in some local bars and restaurants in the countryside it's still cash only.

OPEN HOURS

Banks are open Monday–Friday 8am–2:30pm and Saturday 9:45am–noon. **Government offices** are open 8am–5pm. **Shops** in San Juan are generally open Monday–Saturday 9am–6pm, without a lunch or siesta break. In and around the luxury hotels of Condado and Isla Verde, the hours tend to be a bit longer. Many shops are closed on a Sunday, even in the main tourist centers. **Museums** and most **tourist attractions** are generally open 9am–5pm daily, though many are closed during holidays. Many museums are closed on the Monday and Tuesday following holiday weekends.

POLICE

In Puerto Rico, **911** is the standard emergency number. The number for the police in San Juan is 343-2020. Police cars make regular patrols in the Condado/Isla Verde area, and a special tourist police force cruises the area on bicycles.

POST OFFICES

The postal service in Puerto Rico is linked with the US mainland and service takes only a couple of days longer than from mainland destinations. Post offices are open Monday–Friday 8:30am–4:30pm, Saturday 8am–noon. San Juan's main post office is on Plaza de Hostos. All hotels will post mail for you, and many sell stamps, at a small premium.

Regular postcards to the US cost 20¢, to Canada 46¢, and to other destinations 60¢. Standard letters are 32¢ to the US, 46¢ for the first ½oz to Canada, and 60¢ for the first ½oz to other destinations.

PUBLIC HOLIDAYS

Puerto Rico has a number of national holidays, many of which center around religious festivals. All US federal holidays are also observed. In addition to these national celebrations, each town has its own feast or saint's day, harvest festival, or other official occasion for having a parade and lots of community fun.

1 January	*New Year's Day*
6 January	*Three Kings Day*
15 January	*Martin Luther King's Birthday*
February	*President's Day*
22 March 22	*Emancipation Day*
March/April	*Holy Week; major celebrations on Holy Thursday, Good Friday, and Easter Monday*
May	*Memorial Day (last weekend)*
June	*San Juan Bautista Day*
4 July	*US Independence Day*
17 July	*Luis Muñoz Rivera's Birthday*
September	*Labor Day (first weekend)*
12 October	*Columbus Day*
October	*Virgin Islands-Puerto Rico Friendship Day; Hurricane Thanksgiving Day*
11 November	*Veterans Day*
19 November	*Discovery Day*
November	*US Thanksgiving Day (last Thursday); Ponce Bomba y Plena Festival*
25–26 December	*Christmas*

PUBLIC TRANSPORTATION

Buses and trolleys. Puerto Rico's public transport system operates in the cities and connects the major towns. Prices are low, with most fares running either 25¢ or 50¢. Bus stops are clearly marked at the roadside. The down side is that most of the buses — called *guaguas* — are often very crowded and the traveling time can be very long. Buses A5 and B21 run from Old San Juan to Condado and

Puerto Rico

Isla Verde. Contact the Metropolitan Bus Authority (Tel. 729-1512) for more information. A free **trolley** service operates on the streets of Old San Juan, from Paseo la Princesa to Plaza des Armas. The service is often so full and the streets so crowded with traffic, though, that it's usually quicker to walk from one sight to another.

Taxis. The *Tourismo* taxi service in metropolitan San Juan is excellent. Outside of the capital so-called *públicos* run on fixed routes for fixed rates all over the island. These leave from the main squares of each town, taking people wherever they want to go (daytime only). You may find yourself on a very circuitous route to your destination as the driver drops your fellow passengers off at various locations in the hills somewhere. It's a great way to see a lot of the island.

Ferries. A public ferry service in San Juan harbor links the suburbs with the old town; ferries depart every half hour 6am–7pm. This offers a great opportunity to view the panorama of the city and bay, but avoid traveling at peak times when the boats are full of commuters. There's regular ferry service from Fajardo to the offshore islands of Vieques and Culebra (Tel. 723-2260 for information; Tel. 863-0705 for reservations; adults $4 to Vieques, $4.50 to Culebra).

RELIGION

The majority of Puerto Ricans are Roman Catholics, but many other denominations are also represented on the island.

TELEPHONE

The area code for Puerto Rico is 787. For calls within the island, the area code is not used. The system is linked to the phone service on the US mainland, and most toll-free numbers can be accessed from the island. When placing a call to the US, dial 1, then the area code. For international numbers, dial 011, then the country code.

All major US phone cards can be bought and used on the island, either in hotel rooms or from machines on the street. (Calls made directly from hotel telephones are usually much more expensive.) Credit cards can also be used, though some hotels charge a connection fee for dialing a phone-card access number or to connect by credit card ($1–$2 per call).

Country codes: Australia 61; Canada 1; Ireland 353; New Zealand 64; South Africa 27; UK 44; US 1

TICKETS

Theater and show tickets must be booked through each individual venue. (See page 83.)

TIME ZONES

Puerto Rico operates on Atlantic Standard Time, which, except during Daylight Savings Time on the US east coast, is one hour ahead of Eastern Standard Time and four hours behind Greenwich Mean Time.

	Los Angeles	New York	**San Juan**	London	Sydney
January:	8am	11am	**noon**	4pm	3am
July:	9am	noon	**noon**	4pm	2am

TIPPING

Many hotels and restaurants automatically add gratuities to your bill; if this is their policy, it should be indicated on menus and price cards. Otherwise, it's customary to leave 15% of the bill at restaurants and 10%–15% for taxi drivers and maid service, depending on the quality of service. Porters should be tipped $1 per bag.

TOILETS

In general public toilets are kept clean. Many of the facilities on public beaches (balnearios) may be sandy and have wet floors by the end of the day. The water in public washrooms is not potable and should only be used for washing. Most hotels have toilet facilities in the reception or lobby area.

Puerto Rico

TOURIST INFORMATION

For information about Puerto Rico before you leave home, contact the **Puerto Rico Tourism Company** at one of the following addresses.

Main office	La Princesa, Paseo La Princesa, San Juan; Tel. 721-2401
Canada	41–43 Colbourne Street, Suite 301, Toronto, Ontario M5E 1E3; Tel. (416) 368-2680
UK	Calle Serranno 1-2° izda., 28001 Madrid; Tel. 800-898-920 (toll-free in the UK)
US	3575 West Cahuenga Boulevard, Suite 405, Los Angeles, CA 900068; Tel. (213) 874-5991 901 Ponce de Leon Boulevard, Suite 101, Coral Gables, Miami, FL 33134; Tel. (305) 445-9112 575 Fifth Avenue, New York, NY 10017; Tel. (212) 599-6262

For tourist information once you've arrived in Puerto Rico, contact one of the following:

Aguadilla	Rafael Hernández Airport, Aguadilla, PR 00604; Tel. 829-3310
Cabo Rojo	Road 100, km 13.6, Boquerón, PR 00622; Tel. 851-7070
Isla Verde	Luis Muñoz Marín International Airport, Isla Verde, PR 00939; Tel. 791-1014
Old San Juan	La Casita Information Center, Plaza de la Dársena, San Juan, PR 00902; Tel. 722-1709
Ponce	Fox-Delicias Mall, 2nd Floor, Fox-Delicias Plaza, Ponce, PR 00731; Tel. 840-5695

W

WEBSITES

The following websites can help you plan your trip:

Puerto Rican Tourism Company: <www.discoverpuertorico.com>
  To search for the best up-to-date **fares** and **hotel prices**, consult <www.expedia.com>. Other sites useful for advance planning are <www.vacations.com> and <www.travelocity.com>.

American Airlines: <www.americanair.com>

British Airways: <www.british-airways.com>

Iberia: <www.iberia.com>

WEIGHTS and MEASURES

Puerto Rico uses US imperial measurements for some things and the metric system for others. For example, fuel is sold in liters, but beer is sold in ounces. On the roads, distances are expressed in kilometers, while speed limits are given in miles per hour.

Length

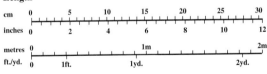

Weight

Temperature

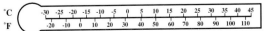

Recommended Hotels

There is a wide range of accommodations in Puerto Rico, in both style and price. The main tourist resorts of Condado and Isla Verde have many large, internationally recognized hotels. More modest accommodations can be found in *paradores* (small family-run hotels) and in historic houses that have been converted into lodgings. Prices at the resorts start higher than the prices in hotels on the US mainland but vary enormously between high season (Dec–Apr) and the rest of the year.

Prices below are quoted in US dollars and are based on double occupancy. Hotels add a lodging tax of between 8–11%.

Unless otherwise stated, standard features include air conditioning, color cable TV, clock radio, refrigerator or mini-bar, coffee-making facilities, hairdryer, iron and ironing board, and wall safe. Water sports includes wind-surfing, Hobie cats, and kayaks (and most other non-motorized activities).

When calling or faxing to make a reservation, preface the telephone number with Puerto Rico's area code, 787 (if calling from outside the US, first dial 1).

✿✿✿✿✿	above $300
✿✿✿✿	$200–$300
✿✿✿	$130–$200
✿✿	$90–$130
✿	below $90

SAN JUAN

Old San Juan

El Convento Hotel ✿✿✿ *Box 1048, 100 Calle Cristo, San Juan 00902; Tel. 723-9020 or 800-468-2779; fax 721-2877; website <www.elconvento.com>.* In the heart of the old town, only a few minutes walk from museums, fortresses, shopping, and nightlife, this recently renovated award-winning small hotel was once a historic convent. Small pool, Jacuzzi and sun deck. Continental breakfast and tea-time wine and cheese. Valet parking. 100 rooms. Major credit cards.

The Gallery Inn ❀❀❀ *204-206 Calle Norzagaray, San Juan 00902; Tel. 722-1808; fax 724-7360; website <www.thegalleryinn.com>*. Renowned B&B run by sculptress Jan D'Esopa in her gallery/studio/home. Within walking distance of all the delights of San Juan, the house overlooks the north walls and the sea. Pet parrots fill the walled gardens and each room is individually designed. Continental breakfast. Three free parking places. 22 rooms. Major credit cards.

Wyndham Old San Juan Hotel and Casino ❀❀❀❀❀ *100 Calle Brumbaugh, San Juan 00902; Tel. 751-5100 or 800-Wyndham; fax 721-1111; website <www.wyndham.com.>*. A modern hotel and casino situated opposite the cruise port dock in old San Juan. Rooftop pool. Fine restaurant and 2 lounges overlooking the bay. Health club. 240 rooms. Major credit cards.

Isla Verde

Carib Inn Tennis Club and Resort ❀❀❀ *Box 12112, Loiza Station, Isla Verde 00914; Tel. 791-3535; fax 791-0104*. One block from the ocean in the heart of all of Isla Verde's activity, the Caribe has a restaurant, 8 tennis courts, a pool and children's pool, gym, sauna, and steam room. 225 rooms. Major credit cards.

Casa de Playa ❀❀ *86 Isla Verde Avenue, Carolina 00979; Tel. 728-9779 or 800-916-2272; fax 727-1334*. Small, low-rise hotel in eastern Isla Verde close to the airport. The hotel sits against the beach and has bar and restaurant on-site. A good option in the inexpensive category. 20 rooms. Major credit cards.

Colony San Juan Beach Hotel ✿✿✿-✿✿✿✿ *Calle Tartak 2, Carolina 00979; Tel. 253-0100; fax 253-0220.* One of the smallest on the Isla Verde strip, this hotel is a good value, offering quality accommodations at more moderate prices than many lodgings in the area. It overlooks a wide expanse of gently shelving beach. Small rooftop pool and sun deck with a bar that's open from late afternoon to evening. Restaurant on-site, and only minutes from many other eateries. Valet parking. 71 rooms. Major credit cards.

Empress Oceanfront ✿✿✿ *Calle Amapola 2, Carolina 00979; Tel. 791-3083 or 800-678-0757; fax 791-1423.* Set on a headland between the two main Isla Verde beaches, this small hostelry is only a few steps away from all the activity of the strip. It also has a fantastic view over the beaches and the other high-rise hotels. Pool and Jacuzzi. Sonny's Restaurant. 30 rooms. Major credit cards.

Ritz-Carlton San Juan Hotel and Casino ✿✿✿✿✿ *6961 Route 187, Isla Verde 00979; Tel. 253-1700 or 800-241-3333; fax 253-1777; website <www.ritzcarlton.com>.* At the eastern edge of Isla Verde, very near the balneario and only 5 minutes from Muñoz Marín Airport. The hotel has 6 bars/restaurants, including a cigar bar and the Vineyard Room, 2 lighted tennis courts, a pool, casino, shops, and a fitness center. The few rooms with balconies are priced at a premium. Parking. 419 rooms. Major credit cards.

San Juan Grand Beach Resort and Casino ✿✿✿✿ *Route 187, Isla Verde Road, Isla Verde 00979 (mailing address: Box 6676, Loiza Station); Tel. 791-6100 or 800-443-2009; fax 791-8525.* Occupying a prime site on the Isla Verde strip, this hotel has a casino and several restaurants on-site. Evening floor shows are a popular tourist attraction. The Plaza Club is almost like a hotel within the hotel, and the swimming pool is one of the most elaborate on the island. Valet parking. 401 rooms. Major credit cards.

Wyndham El San Juan Hotel and Casino ✪✪✪✪✪ *6063 Isla Verde Avenue, Carolina 00979 (mailing address: P.O. Box 9022-2872, PR 00902-2872); Tel. 791-1000 or 800-468-2818; fax 791-7091; website <www.wyndham.com>*. Probably the best hotel on the Isla Verde strip, and one of the most famed in the Caribbean, the El San Juan is set in sumptuous tropical surroundings. One third of the rooms are bungalow-style, the rest are housed in a 17-story wing. The hotel also has 6 restaurants, 2 swimming pools, a health club with steam room and sauna, water sports, a children's program, 24-hour room service, and babysitting. 410 rooms. Major credit cards.

Dorado

Hyatt Dorado Beach Resort and Casino ✪✪✪✪ *Route 693, Dorado 00646; Tel. 796-1234 or 800-233-1234; fax 796-2022*. The quieter and more romantic of two Hyatt hotels in Dorado (the Cerromar is more family-oriented), this low-rise hotel is set among lush gardens on a beautiful beach-front site. The rooms here are finished to a high standard. Two pools, 7 tennis courts, 24-hour room service, babysitting, children's program. 286 rooms. Major credit cards.

THE EAST COAST

Fajardo

El Conquistador Resort and Country Club ✪✪✪✪✪ *1000 Avenida El Conquistador, Box 7001, Fajardo 00738; Tel. 963-1000 or 800-468-5228; fax 863-6500; website <www.williamshosp.com>*. Large resort hotel with excellent facilities northeast of Fajardo. The resort is split into several separate guest areas, each of which has a different ambiance, from busy/family to private/romantic. Both private rooms and efficiencies available. Guests can take a free ferry to a private island off the coast. Golf course, 6 swimming pools, 20 cafés and restaurants, a children's program (Camp Coquí), casino, tennis, night-club, shopping mall, fitness center, and spa (extra cost). Parking. 918 rooms. Major credit cards.

Humacao

Wyndham Palmas del Mar Resort ✵✵✵ *170, Canderelo, Hamacao, 00791; Tel. 800-Palmas-3 or 852-6000; fax 852-6320; website <www.wyndam.com>.* Set in 2,750 acres of tropical garden on the southeastern coastline, this resort has numerous activities for the active holidaymaker along with a resident community within the grounds. 20 tennis courts, two championship golf courses, and horseback riding and diving, along with walks in the grounds. Free shuttle service around the resort. Kids club. 125 rooms, 130 villas. Major credit cards.

Luquillo

Westin Rio Mar Beach and Country Club ✵✵✵✵✵ *6000 Rio Mar Boulevard, Route 968, Río Grande 00745; Tel. 888-6000 or 800-474-6627; fax 888-6600; website <www.westinriomar.com>.* Large beach-front resort with exceptional facilities situated near Luquillo Beach. The tropical landscaping echoes the El Yunque rain forest. Spanish Caribbean decor throughout the resort. Casino, 2 championship golf courses, 12 restaurants, 13 tennis courts, gymnasium and health club, pools, Iguana kids' club, 24-hour room service. 600 rooms. Major credit cards.

Parador La Familia ✵ *Route 987, HC 00867, Box 21399, Fajardo 00738; Tel. 863-1193; fax 860-5345.* Small family-run inn near the Cabrezas park in the northeast corner of the island. Good fishing, diving, and easy access to nearby Vieques island. Only minutes from Croabas beach and marina. Simple but clean rooms, pool, restaurant. 28 rooms. Major credit cards.

Vieques and Culebra

Casa del Francés ✹✹ *Barrio Esperanza, (mailing address Box 458), Vieques, 00765; Tel. 741-3751; fax 741-2330.* An early 20th-century plantation house (now a historic monument), 15 minutes from the capital, which has been converted into a small, informal hotel. Restaurant on site and fabulous beaches nearby. Pool. 18 units. Major credit cards.

Inn on the Blue Horizon ✹✹✹ *Route 996 (mailing address Box 1556), Vieques, 00765; Tel. 741-3318; fax 741-0052.* On the coast very near the capital, this hotel (once two family homes) and its associated bar, opened in the mid-1990's, are the place to be seen on Vieques. The rooms are individually furnished with an interesting mix of antiques and Caribbean art, and take advantage of the sea breezes. 9 units. Major credit cards.

Parador la Casa Grande ✹ *Route 612, Box 616, Culebra 00641; Tel. 894-3939; fax 894-3900.* An old plantation house now converted into a simple parador. Each room has a balcony. No air conditioning, but the mountain air on this island is cool. Pool, restaurant. 20 rooms. Major credit cards.

THE SOUTH COAST

Boquerón

Parador Bahía Salinas Beach ✹✹ *Route 301, Box 2356, Boquerón 00622; Tel. 254-1212; fax 254-1215; e-mail <bahiasal@caribe.net>.* Situated on a pretty beach between Boquerón and Cabo Rojo, with excellent views of the sunset, this small parador has a wonderful setting. The rooms are pleasant if basic. Pool and restaurant. 24 rooms. Major credit cards.

Guánica

Copamarina Beach Resort ✹✹✹ *Route 333, km 6.5, Box 805, Guánica 00653; Tel. 821-0505 or 800-468-4553; fax 821-*

0070; website <www.copamarina.com>. Situated in 16 acres of tropical garden on the beachfront at Guánica. Pretty tropical furnishings of wood and rattan in the guest rooms. Two pools and children's pool, hot tub, 2 tennis courts, and water sports. A renowned Caribbean restaurant, bar, and café. 106 rooms. Major credit cards.

Ponce

Meliá Hotel ✻ *2 Calle Cristina, Box 1431, Town Square, Ponce 00733; Tel. 842-0260; fax 841-3602.* Just steps away from the central square in the center of Ponce. Once the town's major business hotels, it still has a strong regular clientele, though the furnishings and decor now reflect a slightly faded grandeur. Continental breakfast served on rooftop terrace. 80 rooms. Major credit cards.

Ponce Hilton and Casino ✻✻✻✻ *Route 14, 1150 Avenida Caribe, Box 7419, Ponce 00732; Tel. 259-7777 or 800-445-8667; fax 259-7618.* Situated 5 miles from the city, on the waterfront, this is the largest hotel in Ponce. Two restaurants, 3 bars, pool, 4 tennis courts, fitness center, and small shopping mall. 153 rooms. Major credit cards.

THE NORTH COAST

Quebradillas

Parador Vistamar ✻ *6205 Route 2, Carretera 113N, Quebradillas 00678; Tel. 895-2065; fax 895-2294.* Set on a hillside above route 2, with a view of Guajataca Beach, this parador has clean, simple modern rooms. Ideally placed for touring the Arecibo area. Pool, bar, and restaurant serving local dishes and international cuisine. 55 rooms. Major credit cards.

Rincón

Horned Dorset Primavera ✻✻✻✻ *Route 429, km 0.3, Box 1132, Rincón 00677; Tel. 823-4030 or 800-633-1857; fax 823-*

5580; e-mail <INNS4CARIB@aol.com>. Considered one of the finest hotels in the Caribbean, the Horned Dorset is a place for refined rest and relaxation. Rooms have no TVs or phones, and there are no organized activities or water sports. One fine restaurant, a bar, and one pool. 30 rooms. Major credit cards.

Lazy Parrot Inn ✹✹ *Route 413, km 4.1, Box 430, Rincón 00677; Tel. 823-5654 or 800-294-1752; fax 823-0224; website <www.lazyparrot.com>.* Overlooking the northwest coast of Puerto Rico, this small inn has a popular bar and restaurant (also open to non-guests). Pretty, tropical décor. Very near surfing and whale-watching beaches. Pool and hot tub, tropical gardens, gift shop. 7 rooms. Major credit cards.

THE INTERIOR

Jayuya

Parador Hacienda Gripiñas ✹✹ *Route 527, km 2.7, Box 387, Jayuya 00664; Tel. 828-1717; fax 828-1719.* This former coffee plantation in the heart of the Cordillera Central (Central Mountains) makes a perfect for exploring the interior. Wooden decking and ceiling fans throughout (no air conditioning, but the climate is cooler in the hills). Twenty acres of coffee plants surround the house. Rates are MAP; rooms vary in size. Two unheated pools. 19 rooms. Major credit cards.

Maricao

Parador Hacienda Juanita ✹ *Route 105, km 23.5, Box 777, Maricao 00606; Tel. 838-2550 or 800-443-0266 (in US) or 800-981-7575 (in PR); fax 838-2551; e-mail <juanita@caribe.net>.* A former 19th-century plantation house, this simple parador sits in the mountains near Maricao; you can survey the forest from the inn's pretty wooden verandahs. Tennis court, pool, games room, ball courts, craft shop, and bar. The restaurant serves Creole cuisine. No air conditioning, but the mountain air is cool. 21 rooms. Major credit cards.

Recommended Restaurants

Puerto Rico has a wealth of restaurants that offer both local and international cuisine. On any given night you'll be able choose between having a relaxed dinner of classical French cuisine in elegant surroundings or a sampling of genuine Puerto Rican criollo (Creole) dishes in a lively family-run café. Many of the larger hotels have acclaimed dining rooms that are open to the public. Some of the finer hotels have dress codes, although very few expect jacket and tie—"smart casual" seems to be the rule.

In high season (Dec–Apr) it's best to make reservations at all times. Out of season reservations are appreciated any time, but should definitely be made on the weekends.

If you call or fax ahead to make a reservation, preface the local number with the 787 area code for Puerto Rico (add 1 at the beginning if dialing from outside the US).

The following price categories are for a three-course dinner per person, without drinks. Prices are given in US dollars.

✹✹✹✹✹	above $100
✹✹✹✹	$60–$100
✹✹✹	$40–$60
✹✹	$25–$40
✹	below $25

SAN JUAN

Old San Juan

Café Berlin ✹-✹✹ *407 Calle San Francisco (on Plaza Colon); Tel. 722-5205.* An informal café/restaurant renowned for its vegetarian dishes and organic ingredients. Meat and seafood also served, plus a selection of sandwiches made from bread baked on the premises. Try a late breakfast just after opening times when the pastries are still fresh. Open Mon–Fri 10am–11pm, Sat and Sun 9am–11pm. Major credit cards.

Chef Marisoll ✿✿✿✿ *202 Calle Christo; Tel. 725-7454.* Operated by Marisoll Hernandez, one of the top chefs on the island, this small restaurant (only 8 tables) serves imaginative, exotic dishes influenced by several national cuisines. If it's too hot, opt for dining on the courtyard patio. Open Tue–Sat noon–2:30 and 7–10:30pm. Reservations required. Major credit cards.

La Bombonera ✿✿ *259 Calle San Fransisco; Tel. 722-0658.* This café has been serving hearty Puerto Rican lunches and dinners since the early 1900s. Their *asopao* (rice stew with chicken or seafood) is considered the best in the city. You could also stop in for breakfast or for some cake and coffee during a mid-afternoon break from sightseeing. Open daily 7:30am–8pm. Reservations recommended. Major credit cards.

La Mallorquina ✿✿-✿✿✿ *201 Calle San Justo; Tel. 772-3261.* Founded over 100 years ago, this is said to be the oldest restaurant on the island. The menu is filled with both Puerto Rican and Spanish recipes—the paella is considered a signature dish. Lunchtime is extremely busy with local office workers and business people; choose the evening to relish the dining experience. Open Mon–Sat 11:30am–10pm. Reservations recommended for dinner. Major credit cards.

The Parrot Club ✿✿✿-✿✿✿✿ *363 Calle Fortaleza; Tel. 725-7370.* This bistro and bar serves the best in Nuevo Latino food and is one of the places to be seen after dark. The food mixes Spanish, African, and Taíno Indian ingredients and traditions. Live music daily. Closed Mon. No reservations. Major credit cards.

El Patio de Sam ✿✿-✿✿✿ *102 Calle San Sebastián; Tel. 723-1149.* If the Creole and continental dishes don't tempt you, go for a burger—they're said to be the best in the old town.

Housed in a 500-year-old property. Choose between the air-conditioned interior or patio dining. Open Sun–Thur 11am–midnight, Fri and Sat 11am–1:30am. Major credit cards.

Il Perugino ✹✹✹-✹✹✹✹ *105 Calle Cristo; Tel. 722-5481.* Franco Seccarelli brought dishes from his native Perugia as well as the décor for this 200-year-old town house. Considered to be the best Italian restaurant in Old San Juan, it is particularly renowned for pasta dishes. Open daily 6:30–11pm. Reservations required. Visa and MasterCard.

El Picoteo ✹✹✹ *100 Calle Cristo, in the El Convento building; Tel. 643-1597.* The only tapas bar in Old San Juan, El Picoteo serves genuine Spanish olives, cheeses, and meats. Spanish wines, sherries, and ports are offered alongside the more standard beers and California wines. Open Tue–Sun 6–11pm (later on the weekends). Major credit cards.

Condado/Isla Verde

Ajili Mójili ✹✹-✹✹✹ *1052 Ashford Avenue, Condado; Tel. 725-9195.* If you want to try good Puerto Rican street food in a comfortable setting, try for a table here. The main courses are all typical Creole dishes; the portions are extremely large. The décor aims to give you the impression you're dining in an old hacienda. Open Mon–Thur 6–10pm, Fri and Sat 6–11pm, Sun 5–10pm. Major credit cards.

Aquarela ✹✹✹✹ *At the El San Juan Hotel and Casino, 6063 Isla Verde Avenue; Tel. 253-5566.* Award-winning Nuevo-Latino cuisine in an ultra-fashionable spot. Open daily 6–11pm. Reservations recommended. Major credit cards.

Back Street Hong Kong ✹✹✹-✹✹✹✹ *At the El San Juan Hotel and Casino, 6063 Isla Verde Avenue; Tel. 791-1000.* The setting for this restaurant, a re-creation of a small Hong Kong back street, was brought from the 1964 New York World Fair and rebuilt here. The meals on offer are also said to be the most authentic Chinese food in Puerto Rico. Open daily 6pm–midnight. Reservations recommended. Major credit cards.

Chapala's ❀❀❀ *Isla Verde Shopping Center; Tel. 791-3305.* Good Mexican food and strong margaritas in a family-run restaurant. All the favorites are on the menu and everything looks and tastes good. Mixed family platters available—to try a little of everything. Live mariachi music in the evenings Wed–Sun… and it is loud! Closed Mon. Reservations recommended. Most credit cards.

Ristorante Tuscany ❀❀❀-❀❀❀❀ *At the San Juan Marriott Resort, 1309 Ashford Avenue, Condado; Tel. 722-7000.* The wood-burning oven at this award-winning Italian restaurant produces some of the most authentic Italian pizzas on the island. A full range of Italian standbys is also available. Open daily 6–11pm. Reservations recommended. Major credit cards.

Sonny's Oceanfront Grill ❀❀-❀❀❀ *At the Empress Oceanfront Hotel, 2 Calle Ampola, Isla Verde; Tel. 724-8566.* Overlooking one of the main beaches on the Isla Verde strip, this restaurant sits on a wooden deck over the water. Atmosphere and service is relaxed. Food includes fish, steaks, pasta, and burgers, all freshly cooked. Open daily 8am–11pm. Major credit cards.

The Vineyard Room ❀❀❀❀-❀❀❀❀❀ *In the Ritz-Carlton, 6961 Route 187, Isla Verde; Tel. 253-1700.* The Ritz's fine signature restaurant, one of the best in Isla Verde, the Vineyard Room offers the best in California and Continental cuisine. Open daily 7pm–midnight. Reservations required. Major credit cards.

THE EAST COAST

Fajardo

Blossoms ❀❀❀-❀❀❀❀ *At the El Conquistador Resort, 1000 Avenida El Conquistador; Tel. 863-1000.* Blossoms serve the best of Chinese and Japanese cuisine. Sushi bar and *teppanyaki* tables along with regular table service. Open Mon–Sat 6–11pm, Sun 1pm–2am. Reservations recommended. Major credit cards.

Humacao

Chez Daniel ✿✿✿-✿✿✿✿ *Anchors Village, Palmas del Mar; Tel. 850-3838; fax 850-4865.* This restaurant takes the best of French techniques and signature dishes and serves them in a Caribbean setting. Seafood dishes are a strength, especially the bouillabaisse. Open Wed–Mon for dinner 6:30–10pm, lunch Fri–Sun noon–3pm. Reservations recommended. Major credit cards.

Vieques

Café Blu ✿✿-✿✿✿ *(at the Inn on the Blue Horizon) Route 996; Tel. 741-3318; fax 741-0052.* One of the newest and best restaurants on the island, the international menu concentrates on the best quality ingredients with Fish dishes a speciality. You can also order less formal meals such as sandwiches. Eat within the main building or on the terrace overlooking the sea. Open Thur–Sun 6pm–10pm, bar daily 4pm–11pm. Major credit cards.

THE SOUTH COAST

Guánica

Wilo's Coastal Cuisine ✿✿-✿✿✿ *At the Copamarina Beach Resort, Carretera 333, Cana Gorda; Tel. 821-0505; fax 821-0070.* Chef Wilo Benet uses the freshest seafood and other ingredients to create outstanding Caribbean dishes. Open daily 6–10pm. Major credit cards.

Ponce

La Cava ✿✿✿✿ *At the Ponce Hilton Hotel, 1150 Caribe Avenue; Tel. 259-7676.* This award-winning restaurant has an à-la-carte menu of fine French/Continental dishes and one of the most comprehensive wine cellars in Puerto Rico. Open daily 7–10pm. Major credit cards.

Lupita's ❀❀-❀❀❀ *60 Calle Isabel; Tel. 848-8808.* An attractive Mexican restaurant serving tasty standard fare. Set behind one of the liveliest bars in the center of town. Open daily. Major credit cards.

Mark's at the Meliá ❀❀❀-❀❀❀❀ *2 Calle Cristina; Tel. 284-MARK (6275).* Set in Ponce's historic district, this small restaurant in the Hotel Meliá features dishes from one of the most innovative young chefs in Puerto Rico, Mark French. Classical dishes with a Puerto Rican twist. Closed Mon and Tue. Major credit cards.

THE NORTH COAST

Quebradillas

Parador Vistamar ❀ *Carretera 113N, 6205 Route 2; Tel. 895-2065; fax 895-2224.* The restaurant at this small parador overlooks the coast and beach. 1960s décor. If you visit on weekdays you may find an empty dining room, but weekends are always busy with Puerto Rican families who come to enjoy the local cuisine. Fresh seafood is always on the menu as is an *asopao* appetizer (rice stew with chicken or seafood) that will leave no room for an entrée.

Rincón

Horned Dorset Primavera ❀❀❀❀ *Route 429; Tel. 823-4030; fax 823-5580.* The best restaurant in this part of Puerto Rico, and one of the best on the island. The menu, which changes daily, is classic French with a twist. A limited choice is offered at a set price. Fine wine list and a relaxed but refined ambiance. Open daily 7–9:30pm. Reservations strongly recommended. Major credit cards.

ABOUT BERLITZ

In 1878 Professor Maximilian Berlitz had a revolutionary idea about making language learning accessible and enjoyable. One hundred and twenty years later these same principles are still successfully at work.

For language instruction, translation and inter-pretation services, cross-cultural training, study abroad programs, and an array of publishing products and additional services, visit any one of our more than 350 Berlitz Centers in over 40 countries.

Please consult your local telephone directory for the Berlitz Center nearest you or visit our web site at http://www.berlitz.com.

Helping the World Communicate